REVIVAL
God's Way

REVIVAL God's Way

LEONARD RAVENHILL

BETHANY HOUSE PUBLISHERS
MINNEAPOLIS, MINNESOTA 55438
A Division of Bethany Fellowship, Inc.

Scripture quotations are from the King James Version of the Bible.

Third printing, 1986

Copyright © 1983
Leonard Ravenhill
All Rights Reserved

Published by Bethany House Publishers
A Division of Bethany Fellowship, Inc.
6820 Auto Club Road, Minneapolis, Minnesota 55438

Printed in the United States of America

Library of Congress Cataloging-in-Publication Data

Ravenhill, Leonard.
    Revival, God's way.

    1. Church renewal.   2. Revivals.   I. Title.
BV600.2.R38   1983   269'.2   83-15589
ISBN 0-87123-580-3
ISBN 0-87123-620-6 (pbk.)

For Annie, my sister, with love

ABOUT THE AUTHOR

LEONARD RAVENHILL, an evangelist and author for many years in both Great Britain and North America, wrote his first book, *Why Revival Tarries*, over 25 years ago. Many books have since come from his pen, along with numerous acticles and tracts. A graduate of Cliff College where he sat under the teaching of Samuel Chadwick, he is married and the father of three sons. He and his wife now make their home in Texas.

ACKNOWLEDGMENTS

I wish to express my sincere appreciation to Brad and Estelle Jackson for their work on the manuscript for this book. Thank you also to Larry DeGraff for the excellent picture of the Sleeping Sentry.

OTHER BOOKS BY LEONARD RAVENHILL:

America Is Too Young to Die
Meat for Men
Revival Praying
Sodom Had No Bible
Tried and Transfigured
Why Revival Tarries
A Treasury of Prayer by E. M. Bounds
    (compiled by Leonard Ravenhill)

The royalties from these books go toward the support of overseas mission efforts.

PREFACE

Why Revival Tarries was first published in 1959. Now, 24 years, many sermons and seven books later, the thrust of my message is still the same: revival—*God's* way. Now the message is even more urgent, more punctuated with tears, more provocative, more an object of desperate prayer.

After a half century of pleading, praying, preaching, and writing about revival, America still has not experienced *true* revival. We live in a generation which has never known revival—*God's* way. True revival changes the moral climate of an area or a nation. It could change the world. Has not God promised, "I will yet shake the heavens and the earth"? (Hag. 2:21). Without exception, all true revivals of the past began after years of agonizing, hell-robbing, earth-shaking, heaven-sent intercession. The secret to true revival in our own day is still the same. But where, oh, where, are the intercessors?

As I have said before:

When the church gets a divorce from the world
and worldliness;

When we can ignore so-called Christian
entertainers who attempt to combine Hollywood
and holiness;

When we cease from the strivings of the flesh
and recognize that the Bible written yesterday
is also for today and for tomorrow, and that it
and it alone has the formula for revival;

We shall at least have started on the road to the reformation in the Church, which must precede the true spiritual awakening which alone can save our generation.

Why revival *God's* way? Because we have tried every other way. We must still begin on our knees—we plead or we perish! It's Pentecost or holocaust, revival or wrath.

The disparity between the New Testament Church in the Book of Acts and what passes for the Church today is appalling. We need a new Pentecost at any cost! We need the Pentecost-type of Spirit-guided *preaching* that Peter indicated (in his quote from Joel) should continue until "the sun shall be turned into darkness, and the moon into blood." We need the Pentecost-type *results* that should continue until "that great and notable day of the Lord come" (Acts 2:20).

The disciples were promised *power*—"But ye shall receive power, after that the Holy Ghost is come upon you" (Acts 1:8). The power that they received, and that we need, was the power to be *witnesses*, not by lip only, but by life even unto death! The remaining text reads more literally as, "Ye shall be *martyrs* unto me."

Soldiers of Christ, arise
And put your armor on,
Strong in the strength which God supplies
Thru His eternal Son;
Strong in the Lord of hosts
And in *His* mighty pow'r:
Who in the strength of Jesus trusts
Is more than conqueror.

CONTENTS

I have no bow of burning gold
To shoot my arrows of desire;
And yet, O God, I crave a life
That will transmit Thy holy Fire.

I shall not cease from mental strife,
Nor shall my pen sleep in my hand,
Till I have seen God's holy men
Arise and shake our needy land.

—L.R.

THE SLEEPING SENTRY
LARRY DEGRAFF

I have empathy with Martin Luther when he said:

"I was born to fight devils and factions.
It is my business to remove obstructions,
to cut down thorns,
to fill up quagmires, and
to open and make straight paths.
But if I must have some failing
let me rather speak the truth
with too great severity
than once to act the hypocrite
and conceal the truth."

REVIVAL—GOD'S WAY

Where is the hope for Revival—
God's Holy Spirit outpoured
Convicting of sin, and of judgment,
And righteousness of the Lord?

When nothing else is important—
Only God's presence Divine,
When Christians quit worldly pleasures,
Then God, His ear will incline.

Desperate prayer for Revival
Will cleanse the Church by the Word.
Then clothed in spotless, white linen,
The Bride clears the way for her Lord.

Prayer is the key to Revival,
Prayer that is true Spirit-born,
Nights of compassionate weeping—
Intercession for all the forlorn.

Then will the burdens be lifted,
Then all the sinners will cry,
Then all the chains will be loosened
And worldly passions will die.

The lost ones will yield to God's Spirit
When Christians, cleansed, weep and pray;
God's Living Water flows outward;
This is "Revival—God's Way"!

—Estelle Gifford Jackson

I do not understand Christian people who are not thrilled by
the whole idea of revival. . . . If you want a perfect exposition
of 1 Corinthians 1:25-31, read books on revival.

—David Martyn Lloyd-Jones

Chapter One

THE JOY OF JESUS

Joy! What a scarce commodity this is.
There are many who *say* that they are abiding in Christ.
There are few who *show* that they are abounding in Him.
Joy! How elusive.
How indescribably blessed is the believer
    who has his soul filled with it.

Isaiah had predicted, "With joy shall ye draw waters from the wells of salvation." Our blessed Lord in His high priestly prayer requested from His Father for His disciples, "That they might have my joy fulfilled in themselves." Notice this is a "brand" joy—*"my"* joy. He prayed this for every soul that should ever believe on Him—". . . for them also which shall believe on me through their word" (John 17:20).

This joy was not a passing emotion such as happiness may create. It was not to be partial but complete—"may be full." Happiness depends on happenings. I have seen men in the pulpit seemingly filled with glory. I have seen the same men an hour afterwards filled with gloom. The joy Jesus gives is not effervescent, not a high emotion riding the crest of a fatuous wave.

This joy is as real at the graveside as at the fireside.
It does not evaporate under the heat of adversity.
It does not collapse in the presence of calumny.
It does not wither at the onslaught of calamity.
It does not panic in the presence of perfidy.
It does not sour under the test of poverty.
It does not die at the cruel hand of tragedy.
It does not falter in the presence of misery.

Joy is not created by possessions, or by positions, but by a Person—*Him*! Let me add, however, that joy is not an inflexible, unvariable thing. It is not a deposit placed in the soul after salvation without any chance of deterioration. It can stand all pressures Satan or circumstances bring against it; but, and ponder this well, the sun of joy in the soul can be eclipsed by our own disobedience.

Joy requires at least two conditions: submission and service. "If ye abide"—*submission*—means staying put when it might seem smart to quit. It means "having done all to stand" when there is only a toehold. It means believing God when it appears far wiser to believe everybody else. It means defying one's feelings and fears and saying triumphantly, "Thy will be done!"

Joy comes through *service*. Most Christians are activists; they get caught up in some kind of church work. But not all of it is good. Not all of it is essential. Even missionaries find themselves tangled in lesser things than winning the lost. Unprayerful souls soon get diverted from the supreme task He appointed for them. This is why submission is also necessary.

Let me summarize it this way. The way to enjoy indestructible peace and joy is to determine:

1. To do whatever God commands,
   however difficult.
2. To endure whatever God appoints,
   however severe.
3. To obtain whatever God promises,
   however seemingly unattainable.
4. To die daily,
   however costly the crucifixion.
5. To love my "enemies,"
   however misunderstood in this.
6. To pray without ceasing,
   and in *everything* give thanks.

This will give one a healthy soul and a conscience void of offense before God and man. Otherwise we may cry with Joel:

"Joy is withered away from the sons of men. . . . Is not the meat cut off before our eyes, yea, joy and gladness from the house of our God?" (Joel 1:12, 16).

Joy is not in having possessions. Definitely not! Treasures in the material sense can be comforting one minute and killing the next. Investments, the best of them, can fail. Houses and lands are subject to change and decay. They all are exposed to taxation and other burdens. They all may pass in one nuclear blast—then what?

Positions. These are certainly insecure. The top flight executive may be eliminated in a merger of companies. The skilled doctor may be eclipsed by the appointment of some brilliant and maybe brash young rookie. A throne can topple in a night. A dictator lives in constant fear of assassination. The athlete, long the idol of the crowd, may lose his form and be dropped and in a week become a nonentity.

But joy is a Person—*Him*! Joy is maintained by abiding in Him, by believing in Him, by obeying Him. A prospective missionary, long years in training and straining, had weathered a thousand doubts, and a hundred storms lashing his soul; he had survived them all, only to find that when the ship cut the shorelines his "joy" died. Not really. His *feeling* of joy died. He should have searched his soul before capitulating to the circumstance. Not only had the shoreline been cut, the lifeline had been cut, too; his sense of security with his family and the church folks had been severed. Now he was alone, yet *not* alone. God was with him.

Jesus knew the supreme anchor for this joy. The Scriptures say, "Who for the joy that was set before him." Joy?

Joy, hanging naked and burning in the heat of the sun on a cruel Calvary?

Joy, amidst the cry of a rabble?

Joy, with all the team having run off in the hour of testing?

Joy, with no visible legacy to give to His disciples?

Joy, to die framed between two law-breaking criminals?

The joy that was set before Him. What was it? Well, look for a moment at the joy that was *behind* Him:

He had never deviated from doing the Father's will—that was a stupendous joy. If I am doing God's known will right now, I, too, shall have joy (though circumstances may be cruel at the moment).

His ministry had brought liberation to many. Has yours? Then rejoice! Of the thousands of souls He had touched, He had injured not one. What a joy!

He had spoken everything that the Father had requested despite criticism and vilification. What a joy!

The joy *before* Him was:

This was the will of the Father.

This cruel cross which "he endured, despising the shame" would mean liberation from sin for millions of souls.

This ignominious death would mean eternal life for whosoever would believe on Him.

This life lived in constant conflict with the devil would fight its last battle and triumph gloriously.

This humiliation would mean the exaltation to resurrection for "a multitude no man could number."

This death battle would mean that He would overcome "by the blood of the Lamb" and the "word of his testimony" that He was the Son of God.

This "shame" would mean glory forever for the redeemed.

This identification with sin would mean emancipation from it for all who would avail themselves of His triumph.

Christ's defeat of the devil would mean that He could lead captivity captive and give gifts to men—gifts of power and of ministry. His supreme gift would be the gift of the Holy Ghost—and love, *joy*, peace—to empower the Church for world evangelization. Blessed be God, for *He* was and is God.

OH, WONDER OF WONDERS!

Oh, wonder of wonders!
My God, can it be
That Jesus has died
For one rebel like me?
He lifted my bondage
And soul's misery.
The Lord, King of Glory, was wounded for me.

They led Him to trial;
They spit in His face.
He bore it alone,
Oh! amazing His grace!
He bowed 'neath His burden,
Was scourged in my place.
I'll sing it forever—"Amazing His grace."

With hands full of mercy,
With hearts full of good,
My spotless Redeemer
Was nailed to the wood.
He suffered hell's torment,
My soul to set free,
Deserted by God as He hung on the tree.

He died, but He rose.
He extracted death's sting.
He's living enthroned,
My Saviour, my King.
Let the earth hear His voice,
Men and angels proclaim:
"He's coming! He's coming! He's coming again!"

With the saints marching in,
I shall be in that throng.
In the great "Hallelujahs,"
I'll join in that song.
With apostles and prophets,
But best, Lord, with Thee,
I shall live, I shall live—eternally!

—L.R.

NONE OF SELF

Oh, the bitter shame and sorrow
    That a time could ever be
When I let the Saviour's pity
Plead in vain, and proudly answered:
    All of self and none of Thee!

Yet He found me; I beheld Him
    Bleeding on th' accursed tree,
Heard Him pray: Forgive them, Father;
And my wistful heart said faintly:
    Some of self and some of Thee!

Day by day His tender mercy,
    Healing, helping, full and free,
Sweet and strong and, ah! so patient,
Brought me lower, while I whispered:
    Less of self and more of Thee!

Higher than the highest heaven,
    Deeper than the deepest sea,
Lord, Thy love at last has conquered;
Grant me now my spirit's longing:
    None of self and all of Thee!

                —Theo Monod

Prayer is more than a repair kit
for our broken-down situations.

                —L.R.

Bible bookstores are now papered with announcements of Christian concerts instead of revival meetings.

                —Virginia Stem Owens

Chapter Two

GROWING OUT OF SPIRITUAL INFANCY

Many present-day Christians seem to have experienced three stages: condemnation, salvation, and stagnation.

Babyhood is a delightful thing; perpetual babyhood is deplorable. The father heart of the Apostle Paul longed that those born of the Spirit move up to maturity. He deplores the baby state of the Christians at Corinth (1 Cor. 3). In Eph. 4:12, he longs for the "perfecting of the saints," that they move on to "a perfect man, unto the measure of the stature of the fulness of Christ." Further, he groans for them to get liberated from spiritual infancy—"That we henceforth be no more children, tossed to and fro, and carried about with every wind of doctrine" (Eph. 4:14). Such are easily deceived and tricked by crafty preachers.

Paul's concern is that these who profess Christ's name grow up quickly, not because they would be an embarrassment to Paul, but rather that they may receive their "inheritance among them which are sanctified by faith that is in me" (Acts 26:18). No, this was not a face-saving desire on Paul's part. He longed for these believers to get the right of their inheritance. A child cannot inherit riches; he would squander them. So also, the immature child of God cannot claim his right while still an infant (Gal. 4:1-2). Jewels are not toys. "Gifts of the Spirit" are not playthings. Nor are offices to be worn as personal charms for strutting egos.

I stress again that the *perpetual* spiritual infant is an embarrassment to God. God wants us rich in spiritual things. Unless we are grown-up in Christ, we will be a liability—childish and petty, wanting attention all the time, and wanting to be amused. For years, a church in the Southeast has sent me its bulletin. It's a pathetic thing. No doubt its "full program" is considered "Christian activity"; but I shudder when there are weekly classes in ceramics and painting, skating parties, and a host of infantile things that most country clubs would shun. A church like this will never, never be on the devil's danger list.

No church group that knows spiritual warfare has wiener roasts or even passion plays. There is a *real* warfare. I have said before that we are an arrogant, self-styled bunch of believers. We "believe" to the point of inconvenience—and then quit.

I see a local church adding a large room. I am not sure what it is. I am sure what it is *not*—it is not an extension to accommodate an expanding prayer meeting. The local "First Church" has just elected new deacons. Were they elected because they are "full of faith and of the Holy Ghost"? (Acts 6:5). Today, deacons and elders are usually "men of standing." In the New Testament Church they were "men of kneeling"— praying men. Who checks the prayer lives of the men to be elected? Usually no one. In other words, we will choose whom we want and hope that the Lord will mercifully bless us.

Our spiritual immaturity never shows up more than in our lack of praying, be it alone or in a church prayer meeting. Let twenty percent of the choir members fail to turn up for rehearsal and the choir master is offended. Let twenty percent of the church members turn up for a prayer meeting, and the pastor is elated.

The Bible says:

"Let the word of Christ dwell in you richly in all wisdom; teaching and admonishing one another in psalms and hymns and spiritual songs, singing with grace in your hearts to the Lord" (Col. 3:16).

"Serve the Lord with gladness: come before his presence with singing" (Ps. 100:2).

But does the Bible say, "Sing without ceasing"? Or did

Jesus say, "Men ought always to sing, and not to faint"? Yet today we have gone overboard on singing. Some of us older souls remember when whole nights were given to prayer in the church. Now we have all-night sings.

One day, in 1932, I spent an afternoon with Major Russel in the hills of Wales. The Major had been a right-hand man of William Booth, founder of the Salvation Army. Russel was about eighty years old. The old saint's eyes glowed as he told of the mighty works of God in the days when the Salvation Army was lampooned on the British stage—but it was feared in hell and stormed the strongholds of corruption on earth with prayer and the message of full salvation. That was the time when almost every Salvation Army Corps had a four- or five-hour prayer meeting each Saturday night. Do you wonder that the Salvation Army spread like a prairie fire to seventy countries in ninety years?

On the highways I see buses with signs on the side such as, "AAA Church Choir on Tour," or "BBB Bible College Choir on Tour," but I never see a bus announcing, "CCC Church Prayer Meeting on Tour."

A young, successful singer on the top of the singing circuit told me recently that he could earn two or three thousand dollars for a one-night stand. Ever heard of a prayer warrior getting paid for praying? Where are our values? Singing can be a very helpful and comforting ministry, but it is, in many cases, more concerned with shekels than evangelism. I'm glad to report there *are* exceptions.

There are churches with a Senior Minister, Associate Minister, Minister of Music, Minister of Youth, and Minister of Education, but where, oh, where is there a church with a Minister of *Prayer*? Where is there a church with a room marked: "Quiet. Intercessors at Work"? (For prayer *is* work!)

Prayer in its highest form is agonizing soul sweat. Prayer is not just casting off a burden. It is having sense enough, and grace enough, and wisdom enough, and heart enough to ask God to share the burden of *His* great heart with me. By biblical definition, God has burdens that He shares: "My yoke is easy and my burden is light" (Matt. 11:30).

Notice how often the Old Testament preachers talked about "the burden of the Lord"! Oh, to be a confidant of the Most Holy God! The Lord did not clothe Gideon with himself. He clothed himself with Gideon—the difference being that God was in the center and Gideon on the outside. Self-centered men would "use" the mighty power of the Lord—and some do. The gifts and callings of God are without repentance. Men who long ago lost their anointing still minister, using the same clichés and mannerisms. But they are not feared in hell; they are just "clouds without water." Lord, have mercy!

We know by inspiration and by participation that Job was right when he said, "Man is born unto trouble, as the sparks fly upward." Man is also born to choices, decisions, and options.

Decide now! "Choose you this day." This text in its original framework is familiar to most of us: Joshua had a dramatic confrontation with Israel. They could serve the gods their fathers served before the flood, or the local gods of the Amorites with whom they were then living, *or* they could staunchly stand with Joshua who said, "As for me and my house, we will serve the Lord."

But let's put the emphasis here: "Choose—*this day*." I made a choice, maybe years ago, to follow the Lamb withersoever He goeth. That's fine, but *this day* I am challenged to follow "other gods." Vanity may be one of them; emulation may be another. Laziness could have dominion over me unless I am living with "eternity's values in view." Covetousness is a beguiling god. It calls itself by other names—usually its mask is "success" or just plain "getting on." Nevertheless, it will steal this day unless I unmask this deceiver. This day will never come again. There is no market where one can buy old days or partly worn-out days. They come and go, for better, for worse. There is a sense in which I am the master of my fate, I am the captain of my soul.

Slave of time I may be, but there never yet was a master who could enslave the spirit. I can be prison bound, yet be free. I can be crippled, and yet be a spiritual athlete overcoming hurdles others fall at. I can choose this day to pray or not to pray, to fast or not to fast, to speak generously or critically of others. This day I can repair some damage to a brother's reputation or further foul it up. Today I can lay at His blessed feet tributes of worship and praise long overdue. Yesterday's choices are gone, tomorrow's are unborn. This is the day.

Oh, may no earth-born cloud arise
To hide Thee from Thy servant's eyes.

SEEKING THEE

Lord, I seek Thee for renewing
Of my faith and of my love.
Rush and care are my undoing—
Touch me, Saviour, from above.

Pass me not, O holy Saviour.
Leave me not to grope and fail.
Through Thy blood I seek Thy favor.
With Thy grace I can prevail.

Faith moves in to claim the promise.
Peace revives and floods my soul.
Make me now Thy chosen chalice,
Giving drink that makes men whole.

Seeking Thee, seeking Thee,
Touch and give me liberty.

—L.R.

Chapter Three

WE ARE STILL A VALLEY OF DRY BONES

A century has passed since Oliver Wendell Holmes wrote:

Before Thine ever blazing Throne,
We have no lustre of our own.

On that blazing throne sits One who is the light of the world. Think you that when we stand in splendid isolation before Him whose eyes are as a flame of fire, any of us will dare to "look full in His wonderful face"? Think you not that most of us will turn away from His flaming holiness, embarrassed that we were so accepted in a world that could not accept Him? Looking back from that throne over the path of our earthly pilgrimage, the things of earth will look strangely *grim* in the light of His glory and grace.

Our prayer lives will look so ragged and threadbare;
Our faltering loyalty will look so sick;
Our sacrifice so pale and pathetic;
Our zeal like a flickering candle;
Our treasures of earth will look like dust;
Our limping love will bring the tears gushing to our eyes.

At that awesome time of Judgment, "the harvest will be past, our summer ended, and we shall not be saved" from burning humiliation, as untold billions of souls watch while our life's work is judged and a verdict given by the infallible Judge. Will this crisis find us with swords unbloodied in spiritual warfare? Will it find us guilty of violating His commandments, not by intentional opposition, but by sheer neglect or habitual sloth? The writer to the Hebrews repeatedly speaks of "today." Well, this is *our* "today." How long will it last? *Now* is the time to correct the slack in our faulty obedience and slim sacrifice.

I am convinced that the Church (meaning the body of truly regenerated believers) has never faced a greater challenge from the powers of darkness than she does today. We need a baptism of honesty in the courts of the Lord. Honesty means truth, and truth can be painful. We must face the fact that (with all our mass evangelism; with all our compromised, theatrical presentation of the Gospel; with all the billions spent on radio and television preaching) we have not made a dent in the moral corruption of the nations. *We are still a valley of dry bones.* More than ever we need to sing with Bessie Porter Head:

> O Breath of Life, come sweeping through us,
> Revive Thy Church with life and pow'r;
> O Breath of Life, come cleanse, renew us,
> And fit Thy Church to meet this hour.
>
> Revive us, Lord! Is zeal abating
> While harvest fields are vast and white?
> Revive us, Lord—the world is waiting!
> Equip Thy Church to spread the Light.

Let the fires go out in the boiler room of the church, and the place will still look smart and clean, but it will be cold. The Prayer Room in the church is the boiler room for its spiritual life. When holy passion has ceased to move the intercessors in the Prayer Room, coldness ensues, power is lost, and mortification sets in. The place still looks viable, but it is no longer a birthplace of souls.

Many folks have admitted to me over the phone, "Our church is not as dead as some around here, but we are hardly alive, just lukewarm." Even pastors write, saying the same thing.

God ignores the *cold* church.

He rejoices in the church *hot* with the Spirit's presence.

He vomits the *lukewarm* church from His holy mouth.

The lukewarm church in the Revelation was called "Laodicean." I believe this name designates it as a church of mob rule, where everything was decided by popular opinion and majority votes, and not by prayer and fasting. It may have had packed church business meetings, but sparsely attended prayer meetings. (Is it like this in your church?)

The city of Laodicea was prosperous, and the church folks climbed on the band wagon of prosperity. The city had a banking system, flourishing industry, and a well-known medical clinic. Eyesalve was a major export, and yet with irony God says, "I counsel thee to anoint thine eyes with eyesalve." Later He says that, rich as they were materially, spiritually they were "wretched, and miserable, and poor, and blind, and naked" (Rev. 3:17, 18).

The great Apostle Paul says that he had "great conflict" (wrestling in prayer?) for the folks at Laodicea (Col. 2:1). In chapter 4, verse 12, he assures the Colossians that Epaphras was "always labouring fervently for you in prayers, that ye may stand perfect and complete in all the will of God." In the next verse Paul says, "I bear him record, that he hath a great zeal for you and them that are in Laodicea." In verse 16 Paul asks that "this epistle be read also in the church of the Laodiceans; and that ye likewise read the epistle from Laodicea." With all this wealth of spiritual background, the church had foundered on material prosperity and was named by Christ as "poor and wretched and miserable." Today we boast of our intellectual ministries, our endless activities, our stimulating programs, etc., yet I wonder what the One with eyes as a flame of fire sees in us.

Many preachers paint gruesome pictures with statistics on the porno trade, abortion, crime, murder, divorce, etc., but the time has come when judgment must begin at *the house of the Lord*. The painful fact is that "the salt has lost its savor."

Recently I learned that salt may lose its savor, but it does not lose its *potency*. When it ceases to heal, then it proceeds to corrupt. So the lukewarm church is a greater hindrance than the cold one!

Why revival—*God's way*? Because we have tried every other way. Because, instead of healing the cripple at the gate of the church (in the Acts story he was a type of the crippled world), the "Church" is now crippled and asking alms of the world to carry on the Lord's work. How amazing! "In God We Trust" may be on our coins, but who does trust Him? Do the radio and television preachers trust Him for their needs? If they did they would never drag His name before a cynical world in their tearful begging sprees.

I often am asked to pray for the healing of the nation. No! I am praying for the healing of the *Church*. Then the healing of America, Britain and other nations will follow. As the Church goes, so goes the world!

Back to the sackcloth and ashes. With Isaiah we need to plead, "Oh that thou wouldest rend the heavens, that thou wouldest come down" (Isa. 64:1). This much is sure, *we* cannot rend them, and there is no other source of life for us! We must pray.

Men with inflated egos like to call this the "Age of Science" or the "Age of the Atom." It is also an Age of Impatience, with instant this and instant that. This speed urge has even hit the believers. One writes about a man who prayed, "Lord, I want patience, and I want it *now*!" The truth is, there are few who *wait* upon the Lord. Fewer still are they who can say, "I waited patiently for the Lord; and he inclined unto me and heard my cry" (Ps. 40:1). We rush to pour out our complaint unto Him. We forget to wait until He talks to us. We expect fast service to our prayers as though the Lord has an express lane for those with ten requests or less.

Almost a century ago, Asbury Lowrey wrote a book, *The Possibilities of Grace*. In the book, Lowrey explored one aspect of grace, namely, holiness. But the title is challenging, the *possibilities*—how vast they are!

On one occasion, as Dr. Tozer and I talked, he said (soberly, as usual—he was no joker), "Len, when we meet the Master on His great throne, few of us will look Him straight in the eye. We will all want to bow our heads." How true! Then we shall discover not just what we have done, but how much we left undone, how we majored on minors and minored on majors. In that awesome day, we shall discover:

That the flesh had pulled us more than we are aware of now;

That very few of us had, day by day, lived with eternity's values in view;

That we had been content to see through a glass darkly;

That we had traveled with spiritual
pygmies and not craved for the companionship
of giants;

That we had been satisfied to swallow the
predigested food of popular radio and
television preachers;

That we had been satisfied to wear the
faded garments of hand-me-down theology.

As we look back over the track of earthly life, we shall see that we:

Mistook the pond of "church" programs
for the vast ocean of undiscovered
blessing with its hidden gold;

Had nestled in prayer with its comfort
and not wrestled in prayer with its mighty
conflicts;

Had prayed about much trivia and
not known much about mighty travail.

Do you wonder that God shall "wipe away all tears from our eyes" when:

We see our blunders?

We see that He blocked the road; and we sweated,
praying for strength to get over the blockage
put there by divine order?

We discover that we had prayed for strength to live
when He was trying to get us to die?

We discover that we knelt at the cross asking
for a victory,
when He was wanting us to get *on* the cross
to be a victim-victor?

We were asking for life,
and He wanted us dead
that we might "know Him
and the power of His resurrection,
and the fellowship of His suffering"?

Alas, even in prayer we so often are preening our feathers
instead of trying our wings. Yes, from the vantage point of
eternity, the things of earth will look strangely *grim*. The gold
of earth will be as dross.

I'M RESTING IN THE LORD

I must be carried to the skies
On flowery beds of ease.
Let others fight to win the prize
And battle on their knees.

I cannot fight, but I must reign
In heaven's blest abode.
I'm glad that some endure the pain—
I'm resting in the Lord!

There are no foes for me to face.
My pastor is so good.
He says, "Just draw on saving grace
And love the brotherhood."

I am a soldier of the cross,
Unfaithful though I am.
I pay my tithes for His own cause,
But blush to speak His name.

I'm sure in that day of rewards,
He'll give me some small prize;
And my so gracious, loving Lord
Will wipe tears from my eyes.

—L.R.

Chapter Four

TRUTH LIES FALLEN IN THE STREET

"O Zion, haste, thy mission high fulfilling." So wrote Mary Ann Thomson. Another stanza of the hymn declares:

Behold how many thousands still are lying
Bound in the darksome prisonhouse of sin,
With none to tell them of the Saviour's dying
Or of the life He died for them to win.

How, in the light of a burgeoning world population and a half-paralyzed Church, can we be tearless in our personal or church prayer times? There are more lost souls on this planet earth at this moment than ever in history. What a challenge to pray the Lord of the harvest to send forth laborers! Yet how can they hear without a soul-hot preacher declaring that this generation of believers is responsible for this generation of lost multitudes?

Here is some fuel to fire your soul. We in the United States gave the world a crop of false religions. We sowed to the wind the error of Mormonism, plus the Jehovah's Witnesses' lie. Spiritism was received here through the Fox sisters. Christian Science was birthed in this fair land. The Unity School of Christianity was " 'supplied salvation,' as Sears Roebuck supplies overalls, cut to size and delivered by parcel post," to use a phrase of Dr. Walter Martin; it first raised its head in Kansas City in 1889. We gave the world these and other cults, also. Having sown to the wind, we are now reaping the whirlwind. Our youth are captured by the thousands in Sun Myung Moon's net. The Hare-Krishna cult, as the Moonies, finds that almost 40 percent of its followers is composed of intellectual young Jews. And now we have Muslim mosques across the nation. America is a mission field for heresy, and the stuff thrives in our midst.

"Truth is fallen in the street," cries Isaiah (Isa. 59:14). What is far worse, truth lies fallen in the pulpits today. The preachers are preaching what the mighty Apostle Paul calls "another gospel." Men wrest the Scriptures to their own destruction and to cripple the faith of others. Many ministers are happy to be babysitters for believers suffering from chronic spiritual malnutrition. The pulpiteers are happy to proclaim with loud voice to the pew dwellers that they can have a thousand benefits for their one deposit of sins at the cross. The vast array of eternal bliss is emphasized *weekly*. The responsibilities of the soldier-Christian are advanced *weakly*. The fact is, one hardly ever hears the song, "Soldiers of Christ, arise and put your armor on." He fought the fight in Gethsemane and at the cross. We get the benefits and cruise home to glory!

But the Christian life is a battle. Believers on "Easy Street" will pay well, especially to the gospel talk show entrepreneurs who build their own kingdoms in the name of the One who alone has *the* Kingdom.

Just recently I heard a host of a popular Christian talk show tell his million listeners that if they wanted God to love them they needed to give, because "the Lord loveth a cheerful giver." This pulls on the heart strings—love loves to give—but giving to the Lord requires something more than a dollar a week to a greedy Gospeller; it requires that one first give *himself* to the Lord. Giving a dollar for a so-called gospel cause requires neither morality, spirituality, nor sacrifice. There is no danger involved. One would think these days that there is an evangelistic "stock market" in which one can invest by giving to support "our program." What utter fraud! What contemptible mischief! What carnality! What lying!

At this moment the world lies bleeding at our feet, raped by war, ravaged by famine, ripped by inflation, repressed by

recession, and riddled by unemployment. The United Nations
watches with anxiety while Northern Ireland is devastated by
a near-civil war, while Afghanistan is raped before our eyes,
while Iran and Iraq slaughter each other, while Poland cries in
bondage, while Lebanon writhes in pain, and while Central
America is decimated by Communist insurgents. In this
framework of powerless politics, inflated greed, and spiritual
decline, there are just three types of people: (1) those who are
afraid, (2) those who do not know enough to be afraid, and (3)
those who know the Bible.

I am tempted to think that this is the devil's "millen-
nium." He is reigning over almost the entire world. As the Bible puts it, "The whole world lieth in wickedness" (1 John
5:19). Men are scared. Take this example from "The Knight-
Rider Wire," from the pen of Jim Hampton:

> Do you have, growing deep in your gut these days, the same
> kind of knot I have growing in mine? The awful, keep-you-
> awake-nights knot that tells you something is dreadfully
> wrong with your country, with the whole world? . . . Because
> it has just dawned on you that Armageddon isn't just some
> allegory you read about in the Bible, it's real? And for the
> first time in your life the match is so close to the fuse, Arma-
> geddon is actually possible? I have that knot. I have asked a
> dozen of my friends, and they have it, too, and *not one* of
> them doesn't.

Get this clearly, that "men's hearts [are] failing them for
fear" (Luke 21:26). Many young couples (even Christians) are
saying that they will not bring children into this world so full
of madness, possible super wars, threatened calamities, and
shortages in necessities such as drinking water and food supplies.

Why are we plagued with gutter morality? Don't tell me
that the folks enjoying this barnyard morality are not educated. Rita Jenrette (wife of the South Carolina Congressman
John Jenrette, convicted of bribery in the Abscam case) says:

> Congress is a world of thirsts that cannot be quenched. The
> drug habits, the drinking problems, the mistresses, the boy-

> friends, the broken homes, attest to that. . . . Sex and alcohol
> become a convenient pitstop on the Congressional fast track.

Why can evildoers (from the ghettos to the government) stifle conscience, indulge in acts of horrendous violence, defy the laws of God and the laws of the government? I can find just one answer to this reckless living. It is this: These people have never heard *the* Gospel. They probably have heard *a* "gospel."

The Apostle Paul said, "I am not ashamed of the gospel of Christ: for it is the power of God unto salvation" (Rom. 1:16). He lived in a bloody world; the Romans had conquered much of it with the sword. Against this he held the blood of the cross. His warfare was known in hell: "Jesus I know, and Paul I know . . ." said the demons! (Acts 19:15).

Today we have "another gospel" (Gal. 1:6). The cross now is a pretty, ornamental thing in gold or silver, decorated (if you can afford it) with diamonds or rubies. It is a "charm" for some, held not in fear but in superstitious "reverence."

The God of holiness and eternal majesty is hardly mentioned these days. The preachers used to declare with holy boldness to the pew dwellers, "You are lost." Today it is, "You are loved." It takes living men to deliver the living Word. Unless the preachers walk in the fear of the Lord and step out of eternity into the pulpits, the spiritual life of the nation will continue in its descent to weakness and finally apostasy.

St. Paul's unwavering zeal for the lost can be explained, I am sure, by his own words: "Knowing therefore the terror of the Lord, we persuade men" (2 Cor. 5:11). Did he, when he was caught up into the third heaven, see the Savior in His blazing glory as did Isaiah? Did he see the clouds of fiery judgment hovering over evildoers? Paul says to the Corinthians (2 Cor. 5:10) almost the same that Jude says:

"Behold, the Lord cometh with ten thousands of his saints, to execute judgment upon all, and to convince all that are ungodly among them of all their ungodly deeds which they have ungodly committed" (Jude 14, 15).

Do you wonder that Paul does not mute his message about the "terror of the Lord"?

Time was when people went to church to meet God. Now
they go to hear a sermon about Him. If the Lord in His risen
majesty appeared in some church groups, there would be a
stampede for the door. We preachers are at fault. We need a
national day of penitence and prayer for preachers.

THE GLORY YET TO BE

God called to us, His people,
To be His holy Bride,
From out the rest of living souls,
He calls us to His side.
The way He calls is rugged, steep.
The way He knows, we are His sheep.
No blind design, He has the goals.
His love leads to the water holes,
Gives us this day our daily bread,
And hitherto He's always led.
Though dark the way, the path is steep;
He drives the wolves from us, His sheep.
At times the clouds obscure His face;
But, bless His name, supplies of grace
Can fortify 'gainst every shock.
His wisdom plans for all the flock.
Just now the skies seem solid brass.
Fear not, just think: "It came—to *pass*!"

The furnace seven times hotter be,
"My grace" sufficient is for thee.
Your soul is riding out the gale.
Your courage falters, and the tale
Is not yet told; but brighter gold
Comes from this long hostility,
As Jesus calls, "Look unto Me!
I've planned for thee eternal days.
I've planned for thee a thousand ways.

I went through *my* Gethsemane,
Will *you*, my child, bear this for Me?
My back was stripped, I bore the rod.
Will you bear this for Me, your God?
I've planned for thee a jeweled crown.
Will you go through, or let Me down?"
Can you bear up a few more years,
Or will you cause your Master tears?

While Joseph's brothers made a pile,
Young Joseph suffered for a while.
That "while" did seem a lengthy season
With no design, no rhyme or reason.

The brothers didn't care a bit
That Joseph languished in a pit.
They showed no sorrow for his plight,
They cared not for the wrong or right;
But, God was there behind the cloud!
(He does not shout His plan aloud.)
The path through pit and prison led
For Joseph—to the nation's head.

Not then did Joseph weep or groan,
Each step was leading to a throne!
The starving brothers soon behold
A ruler with a chain of gold.
They wept and each his breast did smite
Before one sold to Ishmaelite.
Their brother! with the power of death!
Each man fell down with bated breath.

Forgiving, Joseph understood.
"Ye meant for evil, God meant good!
He did not leave me or forsake.
He knew each step I had to take.
My Shepherd led by pastures green.
No other way could there have been

For me. I proved that He is God,
Endured the dark, and kissed the rod!"

Take this example from His Word
And follow on to *know* the Lord.
Now through a darksome glass we see,
But oh! the glory yet to be!

—L.R.

NOT I, BUT CHRIST

Not I, but Christ, be honored, loved, exalted;
    Not I, but Christ, be seen, be known, be heard;
Not I, but Christ, in every look and action,
    Not I, but Christ, in every thought and word.

Not I, but Christ, to gently soothe in sorrow
    Not I, but Christ, to wipe the falling tear;
Not I, but Christ, to lift the weary burden!
    Not I, but Christ, to hush away all fear.

Christ, only Christ, no idle word e'er falling;
    Christ, only Christ, no needless bustling sound;
Christ, only Christ, no self-important bearing;
    Christ, only Christ, no trace of "I" be found.

Not I, but Christ, my every need supplying,
    Not I, but Christ, my strength and health to be;
Christ, only Christ, for body, soul, and spirit,
    Christ, only Christ, live then Thy life in me.

Christ, only Christ, ere long will fill my vision;
    Glory excelling soon, full soon I'll see—
Christ, only Christ, my every wish fulfilling—
    Christ, only Christ, my all in all to be.

—Mrs. A. A. Worthington

The Bible was written in tears and to tears it will yield its best treasure. God has nothing to say to the frivolous man.

—A. W. Tozer

Ezra confesses Jerusalem's sin with an agony such as if all that sin had been his own. Ezra's spirit in public prayer, his attitude, and his utterances are enough to scandalise all hard and dry and meagre-hearted men.

—Alexander Whyte

Chapter Five

GOD NEEDS NO SPONSORS

Zealots of our faith are sure that they do God service by making exaggerated claims for Him, such as "Faith can do anything!" Why do these teachers do this? Is it to get the listener to stretch his faith a little more so that God will grant him a long-delayed deliverance? Of this I am sure: God needs no encouragement; He needs no advice, no comfort, no sponsors.

The carrot on the stick to the often-despairing soul is, "Prayer is unlimited." This is totally against biblical teaching on prayer. Prayer and faith cannot do everything. Indeed, *God* cannot do everything.

God cannot erase all history,
He has sworn himself to judge it.

God cannot lie. He has pre-committed all souls
to the Tribunal of Eternity.

God cannot forgive unconfessed sin.

God cannot recall forgiven sin.

God cannot cancel the efficacy of the cross.

Prayer will never get God to change His mind about these things. Prayer is *not* "unlimited."

Prayer cannot exceed the boundaries of God's mercy.

Prayer cannot affect souls in hell, despite
all the Masses offered for them.

Prayer cannot keep me from hunger perpetually.

Prayer cannot keep me from sleep perpetually.

Prayer cannot eliminate the battle of Armageddon.

But let the Scriptures answer the unscriptural statements that "Prayer is unlimited":

"The word of the Lord came again to me, saying, Son of man, when the land sinneth against me by trespassing grievously, then will I stretch out mine hand upon it, and will break the staff of the bread thereof, and will send famine upon it, and will cut off man and beast from it: though these three men, Noah, Daniel, and Job, were in it, they should deliver but their own souls by their righteousness, saith the Lord God" (Ezek. 14:12-14).

Again in verse 16:

"Though these three men were in it, as I live, saith the Lord God, they shall deliver neither sons nor daughters; they only shall be delivered."

This same statement is repeated in verses 18 and 20. Noah, Daniel, and Job were holy men, lowly men, faithful men; and yet they had not the power to win the favor of the Lord for others. God had made a decree, and His mercy was to end with those who set up their idols.

"I will set my face against that man, and will make him a sign and a proverb, and I will cut him off from the midst of my people; and ye shall know that I am the Lord" (Ezek. 14:8).

Ezekiel 8:16-18 tells us of:

". . . five and twenty men, with their backs toward the temple of the Lord, and their faces toward the east; and they worshipped the sun toward the east. . . . They have filled the land with violence, and have returned to provoke me to anger: and, lo, they put the branch to their nose. Therefore will I also deal in fury: mine eye shall not spare, neither will I have pity: and though they cry in mine ears with a loud voice, yet will I not hear them."

Our land is filled with violence today and many stretch out their hands to the sun in cult worship. This continues despite the staggering amount of gospel radio sermons each day and the proliferation of tracts and Bibles. Yet millions could not care less. They are walking to their eternal doom unafraid!

The Lord says, "Yet once more I shake not the earth only, but also heaven" (Heb. 12:26). I pray that before He does that He will yet shake the pulpits. Many of our popular preachers feel so confident in their degree scarves and Geneva gowns that they never think to reach for the tattered, sweaty mantle of Elijah. But degrees do not, in themselves, bring miracle ministry. By "miracle" I mean the way vicinities and even cities are awakened from their sleep of death by a divine invasion. This is what revival brings:

Rent heavens.

Showers of blessing on "a dry and thirsty land where no water is."

Eternal life coming to thousands "dead in trespasses and in sin."

Hark to the tramping feet of doomed souls as they march to a never-ending eternity. Can you still sleep comfortably, preacher?

THE HEATHEN

I'm gazing now in the jungle green
With a people whose bodies, not fit to be seen,
Are crusted with dirt and distorted belly,
With louse-packed hair and revoltingly smelly.
A woman now swings her naked breast
To the mouth of a babe who was never dressed.

She sits in a house with mangy dogs.
(The best of the room is reserved for hogs.)
The husband knows nothing of horses or cows,
But boasts his wealth by his fertile sows.
The place is but fit for hogs and dogs
Who snooze by the fire of smoldering logs.

I have seen them crouched in the desert heat.
I have heard the thud of their unshod feet.
I have seen them shake an unwashed head
As they cringed at the feet of their unsaved dead.
O God, it seems to be madly absurd
That they knew not Christ nor Thy holy Word.

They have gone to hell while we slept in our pews.
While we argued doctrine, we denied them news.
We've reclined in plush and saved our knees.
We have had it lush and forgotten these
Who grope in fear in the heathen night.
Had we loved them once, we'd have sent them light.

O Christ, by the power of Thy holy Name,
Give Thy flabby Church a heart of shame.
Smite her cold conscience, buckle her knees,
That she has lacked the concern for these
Who have, generation by generation,
Been lost to Thine own "so great salvation."

O God, on that day, that Judgment Day,
When homes and banks have been swept away,

And there is no place of habitation
For any man in any nation;
Then every man must stand alone
Before the King on His Judgment Throne.

What shall I do when the heathen stand
And accuse that I seldom lent a hand
To save them from pain and eternal woe
And stayed in my ease but made others go
With a message I knew, I knew full well
Could save them from sin and fear and hell?

O God, my God, in that dreadful day
When all excuses are tossed away
And there's no time left to repent and pray
As earthly treasures in ashes lay,
Then Lord, O Lord, what shall I say
For the money and time I have frittered away?

—L.R.

HOW DO YOU TAKE IT EASY?

How do you take it easy
   When His fire burns within?
How do you take it easy
   In a world that's crushed by sin?

How do you take it easy
   With a thousand tribes to tell?
How do you take it easy
   In a world that speeds to hell?

How do you take it easy
   While the church sleeps in its lees?
How do you take it easy—
   Will someone tell me please?

—L.R.

I am distressed at the zeal of heretics and at the amnesia of the believers.

Chapter Six

HELL IS BURNING WHILE
THE CHURCH SLEEPS

Jesus Christ, the "only begotten Son of God," is the most fascinating man who ever lived. How wide-eyed the folks must have been who listened to His amazing teaching! How staggered they must have been when they saw Him unlock dumb tongues, open deaf ears, put vision into sightless eyes, and chase demons back to hell! Men, sent to arrest Jesus, were themselves arrested by His authority. The heathen testified, "Never man spake like this man." His words by His own definition were: "The words that I speak unto you, they are *Spirit* and they are *life*." Fascinated as the disciples were with His miracle ministry, they did not request, "Lord, teach us to perform miracles." After the greatest sermon ever preached by man (preached by the Son of Man), they did not say, "Lord, teach us to preach." Some place they probably eavesdropped as He prayed alone, and they requested, "Lord, teach us to pray!" He alone, by His Spirit, can teach us to pray.

After they had requested, "Teach us to pray," some of them received the greatest opportunity that any men had since creation began: He took Peter, James and John to the Mount of Transfiguration, to a prayer meeting with attendants from another world. (I wonder if attendants from another world eavesdrop on our prayer times?) He prayed—and they fell asleep! This always staggers me when I read it. How could they do so? Did He pray so long that they could not keep awake since they were not used to long nights of prayer? Excuse them this time!

But they had another and greater chance: "And he took with him Peter and the two sons of Zebedee [to Gethsemane] . . . [and said] Tarry ye here, and watch with me" (Matt. 26:37, 38). They were to have watched, and instead they wilted. "And he cometh unto the disciples, and findeth them asleep" (in this, His bitterest hour). He must have awakened them because He said to Peter, "What, could ye not watch with me one hour?" Then "he went again a second time, and prayed . . . and he came and found them asleep *again.* . . . And he left them, and went away again, and prayed the Third time. . . . Then cometh he to his disciples, and saith unto them, Sleep on now. . ." (Matt. 26:40, 42-45).

This seems incredible sloth and lack of love. Yet I wonder who of us can cast the first stone at them. Is the Church not sleeping today? I do not know whether Rome was burning while Nero fiddled. I do know that *hell is burning while the Church sleeps.* "While men slept, the enemy sowed tares in the field." While we have been holding conferences on theological puzzles, men have dropped into Christless graves by the millions. There they will never sleep. Hell has no day, only night—eternal night. It is a ceaseless night, a night of endless torment. To say that the Mormons or Jehovah's Witnesses and others do not believe in hell is a cop-out for the prayerless Christian. God's problem in the United States and England is not humanism, or Communism or Spiritism. God's problem in America and England is dead fundamentalism! We mouth words about eternity, but live and think as if time will never end. Where, oh, where are the eternity-conscious believers? Where are the souls white-hot for God because they fear His holy name and presence and so live with eternity's values in view?

If we had more sleepless nights in prayer, there would be far fewer souls to have a sleepless eternal night in hell.

ETERNAL NIGHT

Eternal night! Eternal night!
How dark that night will be
For millions who've not had the Light
But who had every human right
To share that Light with me.

When we shall stand around Christ's throne,
We'll surely be remiss
That they have never, never known
Salvation through His blood alone.
What tragedy is this!

Oh, how shall I, whose present sphere
Is to be cleansed and free,
Stand uncondemned before Thy throne
While millions die—in hell to groan
For all eternity.

Arm of the Lord, awake, awake
Thy Church, cleanse and renew,
And sanctify, endue with power.
Then thrust her forth this very hour
Thy perfect will to do.

—L.R.

Chapter Seven

WHERE IS THE SALT?

A spiritual revival is not important to the Church and to America; it is *imperative*! At this moment (which I believe is the darkest in our nation's history and, for that matter, in world history) the Church is plagued with inertia. Let the preachers cry aloud and spare not. Let them shout from the housetops the words of Hosea:

"Hear the word of the Lord, ye children of Israel: for the Lord hath a controversy with the inhabitants of the land, because there is no truth, nor mercy, nor knowledge of God in the land. By swearing, and lying, and killing, and stealing, and committing adultery, they break out, and blood toucheth blood" (Hos. 4:1-2).

God said through His servant, the prophet Isaiah, "And I will punish the world for their evil." Then He adds: "Therefore I will shake the heavens, and the earth shall remove out of her place, in the wrath of the Lord of hosts" (Isa. 13:11, 13). Be warned. We are moving into that period when everything that can be shaken will be shaken in order that the Kingdom that cannot be shaken may remain.

This is the generation of civilized beasts. "Educated" men gave us the atom bomb. Alas, such is the devilish power of man that, to satisfy his own greed, he can now wipe out an entire civilization in one night of venting his wild hatred upon an enemy.

Today the prophets of doom are the realists from among the secular and military scientists. Since our pulpits have more puppets than prophets in this crisis hour in history, and since the rocks have not yet cried out, nor the stars fallen from their places, men of secular persuasion have become the prophets of gloom and of doom. Here are samples of what the intellectuals are saying about this day:

> It is becoming more and more obvious that it is not starvation, not microbes, not cancer, but man himself, who is mankind's greatest danger.—Karl Jung

> We are the cruelest, most ruthless species that ever walked the earth.—Anthony Storr (from *Human Aggression*)

> The dance of violence goes round endlessly.—Paul Tournier

Against this backdrop of misery, I find it bitter medicine to read in *The Wall Street Journal* a front-page article subtitled, "An Evangelical Revival Is Sweeping the Nation, but with Little Effect." This, in my opinion, is like saying, "An earthquake shook the United States from San Francisco to New York City, measuring 9.5 on the Richter scale, but no one felt it." Maybe part of the answer to this sad state is found in Bill Bright's recent statement that the Campus Crusade folks took a poll of Christians across the United States and found this horrendous condition: 95 percent responded, "I am carnal," or, "I am a babe in Christ."

Transpose this condition to the secular world. It might read like this: "We have just taken a poll of the crews operating our supersonic fighter planes, our new computerized tanks, and our aircraft carriers—and they are Cub Scouts." What shock the nation would register! Is the Church shocked to discover such self-confessed impotence?

A preacher waving his Bible is featured in many magazines, secular and religious, with a cry, "Help me clean up America." Okay, go ahead. There is no question that "because of the multitude of our transgressions" and our responsibility for the light we have received, no nation has ever needed cleaning up more than the USA. The question is, "Where do we begin?" We believers are "the light of the world" (Matt.

5:14), and judgment must still begin "at the house of the Lord." I dare any preacher to start a crusade to clean up the *Church*. The Apostle Paul, storming the gates of hell, cried, "I press toward the mark." Believers today have the attitude, "Relax and be raptured."

I admit without a blush that this chapter is intentionally provocative and acerbic. I am tired of complacent Christianity. I am declaring "open season" on our smug, spiritual complacency and amnesia. We would rather squat in our rubber-foamed pews and hear a yet more pleasant dissertation on Psalm 23 for the one-thousandth time than hear a man fresh from audience with the eternal God (a man, whose sweat-bedewed brow indicates the volcano in his soul) cry with broken sobs, "Who will rise up for me against the evildoers? or who will stand up for me against the workers of iniquity?" (Ps. 94:16).

Months ago *The Wall Street Journal* had an article on "The Electronic Church." The New Testament Church was not electronic, it was *electrifying*. The Church fresh from the Upper Room invaded the world; now the Church in the supper room is invaded by the world.

The New Testament Church did not depend on a moral majority, but rather on the holy minority. The Church right now has more fashion than passion, is more pathetic than prophetic, is more superficial than supernatural. The church the Apostles ministered in was a suffering church; today we have a sufficient church. Events in the Spirit-controlled Church were amazing; in this day the Church is often just amusing. The New Testament Church was identified with persecutions, prisons, and poverty; today many of us are identified with prosperity, popularity, and personalities.

We lack apostolic power because we lack apostolic piety, and we lack apostolic piety because we lack apostolic purity. Every church in the country needs a dozen Spirit-anointed sermons on Acts 15:8, 9:

. . . And God, which knoweth the hearts, bare them wit-

ness, giving them the Holy Ghost, even as he did unto us; and put no difference between us and them, purifying their hearts by faith. . . .

Where, oh, where is the emphasis on heart purity these days? We have an adulterated "gospel" preached by adulterers, some of them sadly and sickeningly enough claiming to be filled with the Spirit. Do you wonder that I am embarrassed to be part of the present Church which I am sure is an embarrassment to God?

The *Christ for the Nations* magazine, in August 1980, carried a small article on "The Third Force in Christianity." It reads:

> According to reliable sources . . . Dr. Vinson Synan, Pentecostal Holiness, says there are two and one-half million Protestants who have received the baptism of the Holy Spirit and are staying within their churches. Another two and one-half million charismatic Catholics are staying in their churches. This is five million people. This condition has an impact.

What impact? Where is it seen? I am puzzled, and I get no answer to a question which I have presented to some of the topline Pentecostals and charismatics. Here is the question: There were 120 men and women in the Upper Room, and (without our electronic media, our gospel printing houses, 100,000 preachers, Bible schools, etc.) they "turned the world upside down." Now, with the five million Spirit-filled people mentioned above, *plus* all the millions in the main-line denominations, and with some cities boasting "We have more than *120 churches* now with Spirit-filled people," why do we have the greatest mass of sin within the nation (and the churches) that we have ever known? *Where is the "salt"?*

Jesus still challenges us, the believers, "*Ye* are the salt of the earth: but if the salt have lost his savour, wherewith shall it be salted? it is thenceforth *good for nothing*, but to be *cast out*, and to be *trodden under foot of men*" (Matt. 5:13). According to *Cruden's Complete Concordance*, in biblical times "salt was even more indispensable to the Hebrews than to us, as they used it as an antidote to the effects of the heat of the climate on animal food. Salt symbolized hospitality, *durability*, and *purity*. To eat the salt of the king was to owe him the utmost fidelity. To eat bread and salt together was to make an unbreakable league of friendship." We believers have eaten the bread (the broken Body) of King Jesus. He has challenged us to be "the salt of the earth." We must return to *purity* or be "cast out" and "trodden under foot of men." I repeat, "Where is the salt?"

We need *revival—God's* way. Revival—Spirit-born, heaven-directed, earth-shaking, and hell-robbing—is not important to the Church and to America. It is IMPERATIVE! We will be granted it as an act of divine mercy, or else God's judgment will soon fall on us. He will not wink at the sins in our churches and in our nation much longer.

Again I say, let the preachers cry aloud and spare not. Let them shout from the housetops the words of Hosea:

". . . Hear the word of the Lord, ye children of Israel [the Church and the nation]: for the Lord hath a controversy with the inhabitants of the land, because there is no truth, nor mercy, nor knowledge of God in the land. By swearing, and lying, and killing, and stealing, and committing adultery, they break out, and blood toucheth blood" (Hos. 4:1, 2).

Let the pew dwellers respond with Hosea's words:

"Come, and let us return unto the Lord: for he hath torn, and he will heal us; he hath smitten, and he will bind us up" (Hos. 6:1).

God bless and help the man in the White House, but the answer to our national dilemma is not there—it is in God's House, if we clean it up.

I have now fed you with meat and not with milk. Can you digest it? Consider this: is the Bible absolute for this hour, or is it obsolete?

Give me every statistic you can muster about the vileness of this hour; tell me, if you can, the name of every transgressor in this world; list, if possible, every broken home, every stagnant church, every secret weapon that the Communists have for world domination; and when you have done, I shall not shiver, I shall not whine, I shall only say, "Remember, brother, the Book says, 'Greater is he that is in you than he that is in the world!' " If He is *not* in us, then all hope is gone and we had better close every church in the land. If He *is* in us, then let's repent of all our folly, seek cleansing from all our carnality, and then, cleansed and filled, march to victory.

Gates of hell shall never 'gainst *that* Church prevail;
We have Christ's own promise, and that *cannot* fail!

PUT FEET UNDER OUR PRAYER

I walked down the steaming jungle path
Mid exotic flowers and trees;
There were streams and gorgeous butterflies,
But my mind was not fixed on these.
My head and feet were burning,
But my heart burned hotter with shame
As I saw the diseased and degraded
Who had never heard His name.

I thought then of our stately churches
And their softly cushioned pews.
And I wept for sin-damned millions
Who had never heard the news
Of the spotless Christ of Calvary
Who died their souls to save.
Unless there's change, that heathen mass
Will go Christless to the grave.

God, pity our empty fullness!
God, pity our barren tree!
God, pity our long-range blindness!
God, curse our lethargy!
Turn much-used words into action.
Change ease into Spirit-born care.
Baptize us with Thy compassion
That puts feet under our prayer.

—L.R.

Chapter Eight

TRUE REVIVAL CHANGES
THE MORAL CLIMATE

"Revival," according to the Oxford Dictionary, is "a reawakening of religious fervor." (Maybe "of spiritual life" would be a better statement.) Revival presupposes declension, sickness, weakness. Another definition is "to recover, repair, and restore."

True revival is God's coming to the aid of His sick Church. Evangelism is that revived Church's going to a world dead in sin and, under divine power, pulling down the strongholds of Satan.

Evangelism today gropes along on the crutches of heavy finance and super organization, with a star-studded platform. *Revival does not cost a penny*, except, in the words of Garribaldi, "blood and sweat and tears" (he was speaking of carnal warfare). Our current use of the word *revival* is a misuse. We use it to announce the yearly "revival meeting"—a week's meeting with an evangelist and perhaps a singer. Such a meeting is usually geared to the unsaved. But we cannot revive what has never had life. Revival to the European believers is correctly thought of as an awakening, such as the nation-transforming visitation from God through George Whitefield and then the Wesleys in England. Or the earth-shaking move of the Spirit in New England through Jonathan Edwards, later joined by Whitefield. Any true revival can be proven by the fact that it *changed the moral climate* of an area or a nation.

Perhaps the offense of true revival is that:

It cannot be organized.
(The wind bloweth where it listeth.)

It cannot be subsidized.
(It does not need financial backing.)

It cannot be advertised.
(There is nothing more self-advertising than a fire, and revival is fire from heaven.)

It cannot be computerized.
(God alone knows the extent of His power.)

It cannot be regularized.
(We cannot lay a theological track for it to operate on.)

It cannot be rationalized.
(It is a divine mystery beyond finite minds.)

It cannot be denominationalized.
(It leaps over doctrinal barriers.)

It cannot be nationalized.
(Preachers by the hundreds have been flying to Korea to see what God has done in that country. Most have gasped at the packed churches and returned sad that our mechanical services are so sterile.)

Many people express an *interest* in revival. There are not so many deeply *concerned* about it, and fewer still *burdened* for it, still fewer *heartbroken* for it. Yet, spiritual revival is not an alternative for the nations right now. It is *imperative*.

In a recent television newscast was a report that the Episcopal Commission has recommended that homosexuals be admitted to the ministry on the condition that they act wholesomely! Here is an attempt to sanctify iniquity. It reminds me of a scripture—"the iniquity of holy things" (Ex. 28:38). These men who want this monstrous and outrageous sin covered up, will they allow prostitution in the churches so long as the prostitutes tithe? We need a revival among the preachers that will purge the conscience from dead works to serve the living God.

Geoffrey Bull, in his fine book, *The Sky Is Red*, says (speaking of an old man he contacted in the hills):

> I had come from the city, but he was nearer in a bush. Down there in the town, commerce and religion might hawk their plastic Christ, but here in the backwoods the old man's Christ was still the Living Stone. What price then our ritual by candlelight or our "revival" with "ragtime"? Of what consequence our denominational emphasis or ecumenical deliberations today? To what purpose all our parochial routine? Some may choose to guard the graveclothes, but one question still remains: Where is he who has seen the Lord? . . . With pride we sport ourselves as being "with it," when humbly we should seek to be "with Him." Thus do we stoop to a pop-song faith where film and feature supplant the Word of His power. We become all things to all men and then by all means win none. We have the church at parties when the church should be at prayer, and soon the club-centered community replaces the Christ-centered fellowship.

There are some Christians who claim that one main obstruction to revival is "eternal security," or "once saved, never lost." I believe that one main barrier to revival is *false security*. Others claim that "the pastors alone are responsible for the prayer life of the church." Yet the true believers are made a kingdom of "priests unto God" (Rev. 1:6). Hear Geoffrey Bull again:

> Yet we allow our fellowmen to tamper with our highest privilege. Though we have access, we pander to a bogus priesthood. Though saints are one, we cling to "shibboleths" perpetuating schism, and fondly yield to virtual witchcraft, expecting infants sprinkled in the Godhead's name to be the inheritors of the Father's Kingdom. We limit prayer to chanted liturgies, and doleful-repetitions, as if God's mind will change for beads and mumblers. We make the ministry professional and are glad to have it so that we might mind our own business. We let men institutionalize us, catechize us and proselytize us, control our conscience and consume our substance.

Alas, many of us professing His name are walking in theological leg irons. Like Lazarus, we are raised from the dead; yet like him, also, we are bound and gagged with the grave-clothes of tradition and the bondage of man-made creeds. We are selling our birthright—our access to the throne of God—for a mess of pottage called "submission," or the fear of men. I am not trying to incite rebellion in the flock. No, I am trying to stir up the gift that is within us to reach out to the One who "ever liveth to make intercession for us."

Walter Nigg wrote a book entitled *The Heretics,* with this challenging statement: "The history of heresy shows that Christianity is richer in content than its ecclesiastical embodiment. The Gospel holds potentialities which have not yet come to the surface."

I am persuaded that these hidden powers and possibilities will be revealed only to humble, prostrate Christians, hungry for God and willing to shout from the housetops what God is saying in these days of religious chaos.

I'LL RISE AND GO!

I fled Him when His grace pursued.
I did despite unto His name,
And delved me into sin so rude,
And therein forged my soul a chain.

When captive to my own desire,
When blue with guilt and unnamed shame,
His long arm reached into the mire
And plucked me out. Blest be His name!

Shall I leave others in their woe?
Shall I ignore their cries who sink?
Forbid it, Lord! I'll rise and go
'Twixt Thee and them to be a link!

Unwearied may I lift the load
Of those who stagger 'neath sin's spell.
Stab my poor heart with love's strong goad
To battle powers of earth and hell.

Earth's little span is far too small
To barter for the Judgment Day
When powers and thrones and wealth and all
Forever shall have passed away.

Oh, Day of days, when I shall be
The cynosure of ten million eyes,
Oh, may my Saviour say to me,
"Well done!" as my eternal prize.

When unsupported I shall stand
Before Thy blazing bema seat,
Give me, my Lord, to understand
I did the will of God complete.

—L.R.

Chapter Nine

HAVE WE NO TEARS FOR REVIVAL?

"They that sow in tears shall reap in joy" (Ps. 126:5).

This is the divine edict.
This is more than preaching with zeal.
This is more than scholarly exposition.
This is more than delivering sermons of
    exegetical exactitude and homiletical perfection.

Such a man, whether preacher or pew dweller, is appalled at the shrinking authority of the Church in the present drama of cruelty in the world. And he cringes with sorrow that men turn a deaf ear to the Gospel and willingly risk eternal hell in the process. Under this complex burden, his heart is crushed to tears.

The true man of God is heartsick,
Grieved at the worldliness of the Church,
Grieved at the blindness of the Church,
Grieved at the corruption in the Church,
Grieved at the toleration of sin in the Church,
Grieved at the prayerlessness in the Church.
He is disturbed that the corporate prayer of the Church no
    longer pulls down the strongholds of the devil.
He is embarrassed that the Church folks no longer cry in
    their despair before a devil-ridden, sin-mad society,
    "Why could we not cast him out?" (Matt. 17:19).

Our challenge comes from Psalm 137, verses 1-4. The folks

mentioned here were not weeping over personal losses or private tribulations. They were pained when they remembered the former glory of Zion. They wept at the memory of a burned-out temple and their beloved city ransacked by the heathen who had at times ravished their women. Prov. 12:10 says, "The tender mercies of the wicked are cruel"; these "tender mercies" had been lavished upon this people.

These people had hung their harps on the willows because they had tuneless hearts, because the glory of the Lord was no longer with them, and because they were a reproach to their enemies.

Many of us have no heartsickness for the former glory of the Church because we have never known what true revival is. We stagnate in the status quo and sleep easy at night while our generation moves swiftly to the eternal night of hell. Shame, shame on us!

Jesus whipped some money changers out of the temple; but before He whipped them, He wept over them. He knew how near their judgment was. He had listened when they intoned Isa. 35:5, 6:

"Then the eyes of the blind shall be opened, and the ears of the deaf shall be unstopped. Then shall the lame man leap as an hart, and the tongue of the dumb sing."

He had performed all these marvelous works before them, but the bigoted, blind scholars of the day rejected Him and His miracle ministry in total. They saw Him for years, face to face, then they despised and rejected Him. At what price? "Behold, your house is left unto you desolate" (Matt. 23:38). From that day to this, the Shekinah glory has never been seen in Israel.

The Apostle Paul sent a tear-stained letter to the Philippian saints, writing:

"I have told you often and now tell you even weeping, that they are the enemies of the cross of Christ" (Phil. 3:18).

Notice that he does not say they are enemies of Christ; they are, rather, the enemies of the *cross* of Christ. They deny or diminish the redemptive values of the cross. There are many like this today. The church of Rome does not stand as an enemy of Christ; it trades heavily on His holy name. Yet it denies the cross by saying that the Blessed Virgin is co-redemptrix. If this is so, why was she not also crucified? The Mormons use the name of Christ, yet they are astray on the atonement. Have we tears for them? Shall we face them without a blush when they accuse us of inertia at the Judgment Seat saying that they were our neighbors and an offense to us, but not a burden because they were lost?

The Salvationists can scarcely read their flaming evangelical history without tears. Has the glory of the evangelical revival under Wesley ever gripped the hearts of the Methodists of today? Have they read of the fire-baptized men in Wesley's team? Men like John Nelson, Thomas Walsh, and a host of others whose names are written in the Book of Life; men persecuted and kicked in the streets when they held street meetings? Yet as their blood flowed from their wounds, their tears flowed from their eyes.

Have the Holiness people set a guard at the door of the beauty parlors lest any sister should enter to get her hair curled, while a block away there is a string of prostitutes trying to sell their sin-wracked bodies with none to tell them of eternal love?

Do the Pentecostals look back with shame as they remember when they dwelt across the theological tracks, but with the glory of the Lord in their midst? When they had a normal church life, which meant nights of prayers, followed by signs and wonders, and diverse miracles, and genuine gifts of the Holy Ghost? When they were not clock watchers, and their meetings lasted for hours, saturated with holy power?

Have we no tears for these memories, or shame that our children know nothing of such power? Other denominations had their Glory Days of revival. Think of the mighty visitations to the Presbyterians in Korea. Remember the earth-shaking revival in Shantung. Are those days gone forever? Have we no tears for revival?

When the zeal of the followers of Wesley began to dip, Hugh Bourne and William Clowes were raised up by the Lord to stir England again. At the same time, the Oxford Movement was stirring folks against them. Yet Clowes and Bourne, despite savage beatings and persecutions, fought a good fight and had mass meetings with 10,000 attending. They were men who knew tearful intercession.

A preacher cannot organize his tears. Grief for the lost may afflict the soul at what may seem an unreasonable time. Consider the following incident from Evan Roberts' life.

There was not a wandering eye in all the congregation. Every eye was glued on the young preacher in the pulpit. He was still in his twenties. Yet men like Dr. G. Campbell Morgan and the beloved F. B. Meyer had listened enraptured at the young preacher. The prophet's mantle was upon him. His words burned like fire. The light of another world was in his eyes. This was not just the flaming oratory of the Welsh. This particular night "unction"—that divine accolade—touched this preacher with an unusual compassion and fervor. Let an eyewitness of this solemn event tell us what happened:

> His soul seemed to be saturated through and through with the spirit of prayer. I am a living witness of this incident that this prayer was answered in a terrifying way. Falling on the floor in the pulpit, he moaned like one mortally wounded, while his tears flowed incessantly, his fine physical frame shook under the crushing soul-anguish.
>
> No one was allowed to touch him. Those seated close to him frustrated any attempt at assistance which many willing hands would have gladly rendered. The majority of us were petrified with fear in the presence of such uncontrollable grief. What did it mean? What good could possibly accrue from such manifestations in overcrowded meetings? Thoughts of this nature agitated our minds.
>
> No one doubted the transparent sincerity of the man, however mysterious the happenings. When Evan Roberts stood before the congregation again, his face seemed transfigured. It was patent to all that he had passed through an experience that was extremely costly. No one who witnessed that scene would vote for a repetition. One wonders whether such hallowed occurrences should be chronicled.

David Matthews reported this solemnizing event in his book, *I Saw the Welsh Revival* (p. 41).* This was Evan Roberts' public Gethsemane. I am sure that he often had such encounters with soul agony in the privacy of his prayer closet. What a pity that our seminary men are not acquainted with this kind of soul-shaking prayer. In the nation-shaking Welsh Revival, Matthews tells us that "even the little children between nine and twelve years of age prayed with wisdom and fluency that sounded uncanny." There are records of preteenage children praying with tears at Herrnhut where the Moravian Revival was born in 1732.

Jonathan Edwards is usually associated with severity and a stone-faced approach to his listeners as he scathed them with his sermons. When it was announced that there would be a documentary on television about Jonathan Edwards, I took time to listen. The narrator was a self-confident, almost cocky, young woman. She seemed, as Churchill once said, "Inebriated with the exuberance of her own verbosity." She spoke as though she were there when the famous sermon, "Sinners in the Hand of an Angry God," was preached. Maybe she was over-happy at the thought that she was enlightening her vast television audience. The woman scorned Edwards' lacerating words, dullness and monotonous dirge, as fervently as he had preached the offending message. In her opinion, he was brutal in assailing the hearers' minds with his scorching pictures of sinners dropping into a Christless eternity.

All-in-all, Edwards never gained the popularity of his contemporary, George Whitefield. Perhaps Edwards' sermons were too carefully worded, too logical, too meticulous in their expression, too intellectually superior for his hearers. Yet this superior preacher frequently wept as he opened his grieving heart over the sinners of his day. And he gained his place in history by making an unforgettable mark through his preaching.

*Used by permission, Moody Bible Institute of Chicago.

These great Revivalists—Evan Roberts of Wales, Jonathan Edwards of New England, and George Whitefield of England and America—were all great reapers in public because they were all great *weepers* in private.

Dr. Richard Lovelace of Gordon-Cornwell Theological Seminary reminded a workshop audience that Cotton Mather devoted 490 days and nights in intercession for revival in New England. Mather died in 1727 just prior to the First Great Awakening. Dr. Lovelace noted, "Where prayer is, revival cannot be far behind."

Preacher, is your heart crushed over the sin of your people and the staggering sin worldwide?

Oh, for a generation of preachers who will daringly and desperately pray with Jeremiah:

"Oh that my head were waters, and mine eyes a fountain of tears, that I might weep day and night for the slain of the daughter of my people!" (Jer. 9:1).

IN THY STOREHOUSE

There are riches in Thy storehouse,
But my Lord we are so poor.
There is power in Thy storehouse,
But the cripple clothes our door.

There is wisdom in Thy storehouse,
But in ignorance we grope.
There's revival in Thy storehouse,
But we've millions without hope.

There is freedom in Thy storehouse,
But Thy people are so bound.
There is glory in Thy storehouse,
But it does not shine around.

There is love within Thy storehouse,
But Thy people are so dry.
There's compassion in Thy storehouse—
Then, my Saviour, why, oh, why
Are Thy people stony-hearted
And our eyes so desert dry?

—L.R.

Chapter Ten

JOEL STILL CRIES: "SOUND AN ALARM!"

Centuries before the Apostle Paul wrote, "For if the trumpet gives an uncertain sound, who shall prepare himself to the battle?" (1 Cor. 14:8), Joel knew the peril of muting the blast that his or any other prophet's message would have. Prophets were not concerned with their pedigree. They were concerned with purity. A modern preacher says that the writings of Joel are as sublime as those of the major prophet Isaiah or the majestic verse of Habakkuk. Joel would have had no ears for such flattery. He was thinking God's thoughts after Him. Like other prophets, he sees history pre-written. Dr. Feinberg in his *Ezekiel* says, "A prophet without a vision from God would be false; and a vision without a prophet to herald the Lord's message to man would be useless."

Prophets ate the bread of affliction and drank their tears. They were considered bearded eccentrics, calamity howlers, and a needless irritation. To speak of a "popular" prophet is an anachronism. There were a few folks who valued the prophetic word, however painful it was to heart and conscience. They saw this herald of God as at least an act of mercy, a sign that the Lord had not forgotten them. He still had a word for them. Joel, like other prophets, was almost a lone, shining star in a sky of otherwise total blackness.

This much I do know about these select men called prophets:

"For the prophecy came not in old time by the will of man: but holy men *of God spake as they were moved by the Holy Ghost"* (2 Pet. 1:21).

Joel was one of these men of old. He had been to God's school of silence; he was not the son of a prophet. Joel moves me deeply, even to tears, because I know that the volcano of truth burning within him was hard to deliver.

In his entry on Ezra in his book *Bible Characters*, Alexander Whyte says, "If you would move me with your preaching, or with your praying, or with your singing, *first be moved yourself.*" My friend and neighbor, David Wilkerson, after reading my copy of the book, penciled at the side of that quote, "You must be serious to be taken seriously."

I am deeply disturbed when young men write to me saying, "I am a prophet of the Lord." Prophets are not self-proclaimed. They do not strut. They do not seek a place in public where they can shine their self-made halo. No man takes this awesome honor to himself. And opposition never alarms the true prophet. He cries before God and, therefore, does not need a shoulder to cry on. The prophets all have the same assurance: "The word of the Lord came unto me."

God revealed to Joel the magnitude of his task. He was to tell of a coming calamity, unprecedented in history: "Hear this, ye old men, and give ear, all ye inhabitants of the land. *Hath this been in your days, or even in the days of your fathers?*" (Joel 1:2). The sins of Judah were greater at this time than ever before; therefore, the greater judgment would fall.

God underlined this truth to Joel. This would be a landmark judgment: "Tell ye your children of it, and let your children tell their children, and their children another generation" (Joel 1:3). In that day God took cognizance of the people's sin. He does the same today. Those people lived in a time of limited revelation. Now we have the whole counsel of God, with dozens of versions of the New Testament to help our feeble faith and sick service. Woe unto us!

Much that Joel speaks of is paralleled in our day, including the drunkards. Joel 1:5 says, "Awake, ye drunkards, and weep; and howl, all ye drinkers of wine." Drunkards are a curse all over the world. We have millions of these self-destroying souls around us. The Surgeon General warns that smoking is dangerous. But who warns against the dangers of booze? I am told that we have at least one *Christian* brewer! Since when did damnation through drink harmonize with salvation by faith?

The word of the Lord to Joel was, "Blow ye the trumpet in Zion, and sound an alarm in my holy mountain: let all the inhabitants of the land tremble: for the day of the Lord cometh, for it is nigh at hand" (Joel 2:1).

Just what is this day like? Joel described it:

"Alas for the day! for the day of the Lord is at hand, and as a destruction from the Almighty shall it come" (Joel 1:15).

"A day of darkness and of gloominess, a day of clouds and of thick darkness" (Joel 2:2).

"And the Lord shall utter his voice before his army: for his camp is very great: for he is strong that executeth his word: for the day of the Lord is great and very terrible; and who can abide it?" (Joel 2:11).

Our old master in England, Samuel Chadwick, wrote, "The world will never believe in a religion in which there is no power. A rationalized faith, a socialized church, and a moralized gospel may gain applause, but they awaken no conviction and win no converts."

This is the hour to sound the alarm again. The things that Dr. Chadwick mentions are with us.

A Christian magazine recently devoted an entire issue to revival. There was little depth to the articles by different preachers. What alarmed me most was that only one of the writers gave any space to the message of Joel. Another magazine aired a message on Joel, but it was mostly about the *thrills* of this "minor" prophet's message.

The average Bible conference usually has messages by Dr. A on Romans and by Dr. B on Ephesians. But as yet, after years of attending these conferences, I have not heard any of the tormenting truths of Joel expounded.

Why are we afraid of Joel? Is he so offensive? Does his message set our teeth on edge? Does he leave us with an ache in the pit of the stomach because of our neglect of his God-inspired message? Are we guilt-stricken that we have "turned every one to his own way" in our methods of evangelism? Are we embarrassed that we no longer function in the spiritual dimension of which Joel speaks? Are we intimidated by the clarity of his terms and the banality of our services? Is his message too hot to handle and too convicting to pursue? Is Joel's stress on the preachers more than we can swallow? These are not rhetorical questions. They need to be faced in this hour when mankind is being brutally assaulted by demon powers and false cults.

I have treasured Dick Nelson's friendship for years—Dick is a Spirit-filled, perceptive Presbyterian. We correspond on a very regular basis. Here is part of his recent letter to me:

> I'm still thinking that we have just two alternatives in the final analysis—*wrath* or *revival*. We can have Christian schools; political action; Christian protests; letters to our congressmen; food storage; moving to the country; home meetings; bookstores; Christian radio; evangelism; Christian ministries of every conceivable variety; retreats; bigger and better churches; feeding the poor; giving our bodies to be burned; prophecies galore; prognostications; timetables for the future; etc., but unless we have a veritable explosion of the Gospel of Jesus Christ out into the world, the world will explode in on us.

I have used this phrase before in one of my books, but it is still true that "there is a suffocating indifference in the Church to the peril of judgment for the nation's sin."

Joel still cries to us, "Sound an alarm!" Who wants the task? Joel's message is different from that of other prophets. Most of the other prophetic books have a historical setting which is comparatively easy to discern and which provides the key to the interpretation of the contents. The book of Joel is an exception. Its events are not recorded elsewhere. No king of Judah or Israel is named. No great empire (Assyrian, Babylonian, or Persian) is mentioned.

Search for clues and tell me if the book comes before Amos or after Malachi. I am convinced that Joel's message is *timeless*. But why sift for clues if the house is still burning with people perishing inside? Why have a swivel-chair discussion about the background of the book when its dangers are with us?

Forget the pews; let's check the pulpits. Is your pastor a night owl? No, not a late-night television watcher. I mean one who lies *all* night in sackcloth; one who can be labeled as soul-stricken with grief that his neighborhood is hell-bound; one who sees no clock as he "howls" and "laments" the devil's dominion over his town and this blind generation. Has he a sackcloth wardrobe for his tearful humiliation that his theology is a paper tiger? That he can print the theological menu but cannot produce the meal?

Joel repeatedly proclaims: "The day of the Lord is at hand!" Thus he refuses to moderate his cry: Destruction from the Almighty shall come. The fire has devoured the pastures of the wilderness. The locusts have bared every leaf. The flame has burned every tree of the field.

This is no coffee-break message. This is no plea for a national recovery of the economy. Eternity pounds in the heart of Joel. Ahead there is a "day of darkness and gloominess"; a strong army will attack: "A fire devoureth before them; and behind them a flame burneth: the land is as the garden of Eden before them, and behind them a desolate wilderness; yea, and nothing shall escape them" (2:3). Hearken to this, digest it if you can: "The earth shall quake before them; the heavens shall tremble: the sun and the moon shall be dark, and the stars shall withdraw their shining" (2:10).

The devouring army that will assail the land has teeth like a lion. Then a tidal wave of palmerworms and locusts will eat the crops (Joel 1:4, 6). To stem this tide of judgment, the Lord demands, "Therefore also now, saith the Lord, turn ye even to me with all your heart, and with fasting, and with weeping, and with mourning: and rend your heart, and not your garments" (Joel 2:12, 13).

All people are to experience a time of severe humiliation. Joel lists the people and additional things they must do to prepare for "the great and very terrible day of the Lord": "Gird yourselves, and lament, ye *priests*: howl, ye *ministers* of the altar: come, lie all night in sackcloth, ye *ministers* of my God. . . . Sanctify ye a fast, call a solemn assembly, gather the *elders* and *all the inhabitants* of the land . . . and cry unto the Lord" (Joel 1:13, 14). God repeats:

"Blow the trumpet in Zion, sanctify a fast, call a solemn assembly: gather the people, sanctify the congregation, assemble the elders, gather the children, . . . "Let the priests, the ministers of the Lord, weep *between the porch and the altar, and let them say, Spare thy people, O Lord, and give not thine heritage to reproach, that the heathen should rule over them"* (Joel 2:15-17).

Do any of our seminaries have a course entitled, Weeping for the Lost? And if a man should graduate in that course, is there an advanced class for those who would howl in grief between the porch and the altar over our sin-saturated society?

Joel speaks a language we do not know. His noncommercial, nonfinancial ministry startles us. Our gospel corporations and bank-rolled evangelistic efforts would shock him. Alas, so many evangelistic enterprises that began in the Spirit are now ending in the flesh. Why have we "gone down to Egypt" for help?

LORD, SEND A REVIVAL

I see the peril of the world, I see it rot.
I see the church and know she has not got
What she should have of Calvary love and passion.
She loves her ease and style, and this world's smile
    and fashion.
O Christ, was it for this that Thou didst bleed?
For churches blind to human need?
For lounging pew warmers who never tell
Of saving grace to sinners bound for hell?

You promised us a baptism of fire.
But here we are bogged down in slothful mire,
Thy people fat, content, increased in goods,
Resentful if we prod them from their moods.
Forgive them, Father, oh, forgive!
Shake them awake! And let them live
Upon the plane of Pentecostal power—
Less enduement cannot meet this hour.

Before You come to take Your spotless Bride,
We trust You for a world revival tide!

                              —L.R.

Chapter Eleven

PRAYER POVERTY IN THE PULPIT

Recent earthquakes have left severe devastation. Our hearts ache for the victims of these monstrous calamities. Yet there is a greater tragedy than these sad events. It is a sick Church in a dying world.

The Church may have to advertise its preachers, its conferences, its statistics—it does not have to advertise its spiritual bankruptcy; it is too self-evident.

A critical sports writer says he deplores the fact that professional sports has become show business. One can deplore the fact that the mighty gospel of our redeeming Lord has become show business also—fancily-dressed singers imitating rock stars, elborate stage dressing to try to catch the attention of a dying world. All this dressing up to attempt to hide the fact that the altar has no fire, the preaching has no power, the Holy One is not in attendance.

There is nothing we need more than a school of prayer. Who dares teach it? Those who have discovered many of the secrets of prayer are those who, like their Lord, have had a personal Gethsemane, those who have travailed in the birth pangs for revival. These are the hidden ones. They never strut. They boast not of the hours they spend in prayer. They wrestle against principalities and powers, and their souls bear the scars of spiritual conflict. Men so often strut in the pulpit. They gleefully announce how many countries they have preached in; they are known in many places, but not known in hell. Or, if they are known there at all, they are known as noncombatants, as being of no serious threat to the infernal powers.

These pulpit stars impress their audiences with their flashy clothing, dramatic flourishes of the Bible, and loud denunciations of the world's sin. Who tallies their superficial record of "souls won" in the presence of the One who alone knows the track record?

We are all unclothed in the prayer closet. Maybe this is why we are so uncomfortable there. Do we shrink from the eyes that are a flame of fire because we know He cannot be deceived? He cannot be influenced by anything except pure motive? He cannot be persuaded to give us our priorities just for the asking?

Our poverty in prayer is the seedbed of all our failure. Here in the place of prayer is where the pure in heart see God. They see His majesty. They see His grief over a sinning Church and a world of sinners paying any price and every price for a smooth ride to hell.

No preacher leaves the closet with a sweat on his soul and offers a world of rebels the feeble utterance, "God loves you," without also stating, "God is angry with the wicked every day" (Ps. 7:11).

No preacher is going to skip into the pulpit with the "good news" that his church won the top honors in the interchurch bowling league if he has come from the closet of prayer with eternity blazing in his eyes. No man is going to fear devils or deacons if he has heard the word of the Lord in the secret place of the Most High. My preacher brethren, we had better ponder the following words by Margaret C. Anderson:

THE CRY OF A DISTRESSED SOUL

O preacher, holy man, hear my heart weeping;
I long to stand and shout my protests:
Where is your power? and where is your message?
Where is the Gospel of mercy and love?

Your words are nothingness! nothingness! nothingness!
We who have come to listen are betrayed.

Servant of God, I am bitter and desolate.
What do I care for perfection of phrase?
Cursed be your humor, your poise, your diction.
See how my soul turns to ashes within me.
You who have vowed to declare your Redeemer,
Give me the words that would save!

—Margaret Chaplin Anderson

I˙ stress again, our poverty in the prayer closet is the seedbed of all our failure. Failing there, we fail everywhere. Poverty in prayer produces poverty in the pulpit, and results in "a famine . . . of hearing the word of the Lord" in the church (Amos 8:11). Let us, then, digest these truths about prayer:

Prayer demands no special dress.
Prayer demands no special place.
Prayer demands no special eloquence.
Prayer demands no special scholarship.
Prayer never struts.
Prayer seeks no applause.
Prayer is often most mighty when it is most quiet.
Prayer defies definition.
Prayer eludes explanation.
Prayer is birthed in time, but it grasps eternity.
Prayer strengthens the weak and weakens the strong.
Prayer touches the power of the world to come.

"The effectual fervent prayer of a righteous man availeth much" (James 5:16). It avails because it prevails!

Our ultimate position as Christians is tested by the power of our prayer life.

—David Martyn Lloyd-Jones

THY GLORY AND THY MAJESTY

Thy glory and Thy majesty
Are seldom, Lord, revealed to me.
My sight is dim, my senses dumb.
I seldom dwell on "Kingdom come."

Men dwell among the things that rust.
We live in time, with all its dust.
I would my interests relocate,
And dwell on Thee, my God so great;

And contemplate Thy majesty,
Concentrate on Thy deity,
Thus cheat the thieving things of time,
Dwell on Thy holiness sublime—

Thy matchless beauty fill my gaze—
And worship Thee through all my days.
And then, ah, then, eternity,
Boundless unmarred felicity!

No more to sigh, only to sing
In rapturous praises to our King,
To gaze with rapture on His face
And sing and sing Amazing Grace!

—L.R.

LORD, EMANCIPATE

These doubts and fears,
For many years,
Have fettered up my soul.
O blessed Lord,
Emancipate;
Come now and take control.

I now aspire
With strong desire
To be a channel clean.
O blessed Lord,
Emancipate;
Reign o'er my life supreme.

Oh, take me higher,
Endue with fire,
Thy glory dwell within!
O blessed Lord,
Emancipate
And keep me free from sin!

Now free from sin,
Endue within;
Give Thy compassion—tears.
Thou dost, my Lord,
Emancipate;
Restore my wasted years.

At any loss
I choose Thy cross.
Earth's values I deplore.
Thy blood doth now
Emancipate;
Thy victory I adore!

—L.R.

The religion that does not summon the world to judgment
before its holy demands and lofty standards has already
signed its death warrant.

—E. K. Cox

Chapter Twelve

WHO SHALL STAND IN *HIS* HOLY PLACE?

My late spiritual mentor, the beloved Dr. A. W. Tozer, listened with patience day after day as preachers at a conference told of what *they* had done or how far *they* had traveled, or what building *they* had recently raised. Finally the good Doctor rose to preach and fired a broadside at the boasters: "I am tired of coming to conferences to watch men strut!"

Men do, alas, often strut in the pulpit. They even get lost in their own eloquence. But who struts in the prayer closet? Who dares to try to impress God? Our unanointed oratory is a stammer here. Rhetoric dies. Here our organizing skill is a dry gourd. Agonizing is esteemed—but who can teach men to agonize? Physical strength does not avail in intercession; soul strength does!

In prayer we are known *only* to God. We do not even know ourselves. How unflattering is our social standing here. All Christian men are not equal in the prayer life. Not even all spiritual men. Spirituality alone counts here. God cannot be threatened. He cannot be cajoled. He cannot be corrupted, nor bought, nor bargained with. The laws of prayer are His. "Shut the door!" No spectators are allowed here. No windows display the prayer closet.

Vain repetitions are obnoxious to God. The conditions for prayer are set by God himself. Duncan Campbell, used of God in the Hebrides Revival of the 1950s, was preaching one night when the heavens seemed like brass. Duncan stopped preaching, and he called on a young man to pray. The "laddie" halted before he prayed to say, "Ach! What's the use of praying if we are not right with God?" He then recited the 24th Psalm. The fear of the Lord came upon many. The "fire" fell and the area knew that the Lord had visited His people.

How demanding the Lord is in this 24th Psalm! Argue as the theologians will about "the last remains of sin abiding in us," yet God says we cannot "ascend the hill of the Lord" (come into His holy presence) in an unholy state. "Who shall stand in his holy place?" God gives the answer: "He that hath clean hands and a pure heart" (Ps. 24:4). Without holiness, "no man shall see the Lord" (Heb. 12:14).

The "hands" refer to our contact with the world. The professing Christian employer who exploits his workers, exacting the last ounce of their energy to grind his mills, sabotages his own prayers. God demands clean hands. Hands with no grime or greed upon them. Hands not fouled with grasping illegal gain. Hands not caught in other people's pockets stealing tithes and offerings for one's personal ambitions though they be covered with spiritual phrases.

Then there is the pure "heart." God demands this in approaching His holy eternal throne. Our desires must be pure, our purpose pure. Our hearts must be purified from unbelief; our sole ambition must be to see Him glorified at any cost to us.

The "effectual fervent prayer" can come only from "a righteous man" (James 5:16). Redemption means that we are cleansed, and not only *accounted* righteous, but *made* righteous. The slick phrase, "God does not see me as a sinning saint, He sees me through Christ," will not pass muster here. Neither will the cop-out, "Christians aren't perfect, just forgiven." "But as he which hath called you is holy, so be ye holy" (1 Pet. 1:15). And hear John: "He that doeth righteousness is righteous, *even as he is righteous*" (1 John 3:7).

In my days in England there was a preachers' forum in the Methodist Church on Oldham Street, Manchester. I visited it often. The preaching "greats" held court there. Sangster of

Westminster Central Hall was a favorite of many. Others preferred Dr. D. Martyn Lloyd-Jones of Westminster Chapel. Dr. G. Campbell Morgan drew crowds. Dr. Black of Edinburgh, and others—each had his distinct style of presenting the Word. Yet, I remember their style in prayer, also. The men shallow in prayer were shallow in preaching—oratory notwithstanding.

I deplore the poverty of pulpit praying today. Often the preachers give this jewel of prayer to an unprepared deacon. "After this hymn, we will ask Deacon Smith to lead us in prayer." Deacon Smith should have been given a week's notice to prepare his soul for prayer. The usual prayer is trite, unintelligent, and unconvincing. It goes something like this: "Lord, bless us this day. We thank You for this church and for the pastor. Bless the choir as they sing, and may some person be saved, for Jesus' sake." This is almost unpardonable.

Joseph Parker was a man mighty in the Scriptures. He was mighty in prayer, also. Preachers would profit from meditating on the prayers of this man of God. These are now in print through The Great Commission Prayer League, Leesburg, Florida. The book is entitled *Book of Uncommon Prayer*. He will lift you from the dust of earth to heavenly places in Christ Jesus. He had visions and authority in prayer. He prayed with purpose, with power, with passion, and with pleadings that are rare.

The temperature goes up or down after the pulpit prayer. The preacher who touches God in prayer touches the hearts of the people who hear the prayer.

MY PRAYER FOR PREACHERS

Eternal Father,

In the majesty of Thy glory,
   look down in mercy on these men.

As they fall before Thee in prayer,
   be pleased to fall upon them in power!

As they enter their seclusion as preachers,
   may they emerge from it as prophets.

According to Your promise,
   give them a new heart.

According to Your Holy Word,
   put a new spirit within them.

Anoint their eyes with holy eyesalve
   that they may see what heretofore they have not seen.

Unstop their ears that they may hear Your voice
   in a way You could not previously speak to them.

Touch their lips with a live coal from the altar of eternity
   that they may step back into time
   like men who have tasted the powers of the world to come.

Grant that their theology
   may become almost a theophany.

In these days of Noah-like society,
   when the earth again is corrupt before Thee
   and when violence has become a way of life,
   and sexual immorality a sport;
   when iniquity is legislated
   and unborn babes are mutilated in the womb;
   in this dread hour, challenging Thee to judge us,
   grant these men a compassion
   and a passion, motivated by the love of Thy Son,
   for doomed humanity.

We tremble as we see
    the over-blest, over-fed, over-come nations
    wallow in sin
    on the brink of destruction;

As we see that
    the law of the day is lawlessness,
    the faith of the day is faithlessness,
    the philosophy of the day is hopelessness,
    the evident condition of the Church is powerlessness.

In this unprecedented state of moral anarchy
and spiritual debility,

Let these men not dare to see the faces of men again
until they are renewed in the Holy Ghost.

If these men are not the men to shake the nation
    before The King comes,
    then in mercy find such men to shake earth and hell,
    and fill heaven with praise
    that He has seen of the travail of His soul
    to His satisfaction.

These things I ask
    in the name of and for the glory of
    thine only begotten Son,
    the only Saviour of men,
    Jesus Christ our Lord,

        Amen.

—L.R.

PRAYER IS

There are, I am sure, acres of undiscovered truth about prayer in the Bible.

Prayer is the most unexplored area of the Christian life.
Prayer is the most powerful weapon of the Christian life.
Prayer is the most hell-feared battle in the Christian life.
Prayer is the most secret device of the Christian life.
Prayer is the most underestimated power in the Christian life.
Prayer is the most untaught truth in the Christian life.
Prayer is the most demanding exercise in the Christian life.
Prayer is the most neglected responsibility in the Christian life.
Prayer is the most conquering outreach in the Christian life.
Prayer is the most opposed warfare in the Christian life.
Prayer is the most far-reaching ministry in the Christian life.

—L.R.

Chapter Thirteen

PRAYING IN THE HOLY GHOST

I shall, I believe, be eternally grateful that my father took me to a night of prayer when I was just 14 years of age. Dad was a street-corner preacher. He and his partner, "Hell-Fire Naylor," had been rescued from the pit of sin; and they never forgot God's infinite mercy to them. Battle they did at street corners, telling the old, old story of Jesus and His love. They battled in prayer, also. The other men at that momentous prayer meeting were Walter Dacre and Albert Barnes (not the commentator). I sensed at once, as these men prayed with tears and travail, that they had three things in them: faith, fire, and fight!

This was my first front-line view of a spiritual battle. These men sweat, wept, and called loudly upon the name of the Lord as though He were deaf, and yet with confidence that He was hearing. There were many great answers. This type of prayer seems to be lost in this day of flabby faith and shallow spirituality. Oh, that it might return! I went to a number of half nights of prayer with this team of men—I begged to go. Here was life, liberty, and love! From that night to this I have tried to pray. Like all others, I shall never graduate in this school, the School of Intercession.

If the Lord offered me just one outstanding ministry—say, for example:

The offer of a full knowledge of His word and
a greater power to proclaim it than had Spurgeon;

Or the offer of the most sensational healing ministry;

Or the offer of the spiritual ability to raise up a new denomination;

Or the offer of the loan of Elijah's mantle in prayer—

I would choose the latter.

I would like to pray as Elijah prayed. I would like to be feared in hell as Paul was feared. Demons testified, "Jesus I know, and Paul I know; but who are ye?" (Acts 19:15). What a shock if, at the Judgment Seat of Christ, the devil says, "I've never heard of that preacher"!

I'm of the opinion that the devil has a list of the "Ten Most Wanted Men." There are men he fears. Would you like to be one of them?

> Oh, to pray so as to be known in hell!
> Oh, to pray so that demons have to quit their prey!
> Oh, to cause pandemonium in perdition when we intercede!
> Oh, to liberate the captives when we make intercessions with tears!
> Oh, to push the devil around instead of him pushing the Church around!
> Oh, to know the groanings that cannot be uttered! Some say that this is praying in tongues—not so in my reckoning. If the groanings cannot be uttered audibly by the Spirit, I am sure they cannot be uttered by me! Hannah prayed, "but her voice was not heard" (1 Sam. 1:13).

George Jeffreys, the great evangelist who shook areas of England during the 1930s, said that he prayed in English; if that seemed inadequate, he prayed in his more expressive native tongue, Welsh; if that failed, he prayed in tongues.

But there is another stage—praying in the Holy Ghost. This is the highest form of prayer. It is inner groanings, it is inner grief, it is totally spiritual, and it is weakening to the flesh—but devastating to the powers of darkness. Did you ever hear anyone pray with a holy anointing that seemed to shake the place? Well, there is a step in prayer beyond this. It is painful to experience. Once, in a little town in Wales, I witnessed a woman travailing in prayer. It could not have been more painful and awesome had she been giving birth naturally and going down to the gates of death to bring forth life. This is what praying in the Holy Ghost is about—at least in the context of revival.

As God is my witness, I want to pray with groanings "that cannot be uttered." I want to be taught what cannot be taught—only *caught* as the Spirit anoints.

Lord, I tearfully ask:

Teach me to pray with groanings so that there are earthquakes in hell.

Teach me the groanings of the Spirit until angels stand in awe.

Teach me Spirit-born intercession that changes history.

Teach me the birth pangs of the Holy Ghost until hell-shaking revival is born.

Lead me into travail that will hold back divine judgment from the nations for a little season.

Let me be a living sacrifice on the altar of prayer, "bleeding to bless," until flood tides of mercy sweep the nations.

Lord, break my heart in intercession until my eyes, like those of Jeremiah, are a fountain of tears weeping for the slain of an educated, but spiritually dead, people.

Dead sermons are unpardonable; dead prayers are even worse. If there are degrees of death in a service, usually the "deadest" part is the offering of the pulpit prayer. Seldom does the Spirit fall while the pulpit prayer is offered. Prayer is the key to the service. Lord, teach preachers to pray!

POUR THYSELF THROUGH ME

Spirit of the living God, pray Thy mind through me.
Nothing less than Spirit-power do I ask of Thee.
Purge me, urge me, guide me, hide me.
Spirit of the living God, pray Thy mind through me.

Power of the eternal God, flow Thy power through me.
Holy, Pentecostal power do I ask of Thee.
Lowly, holy, for Thy glory—
Power of the eternal God, flow Thy power through me.

Mercy of the living God, channel love through me.
Nothing less than Calvary love meets the need for me.
Love that's burning, love that's yearning—
Mercy of the living God, channel love through me.

Grace of God, eternal grace, reach the lost through me.
Tenderness for every race do I ask of Thee.
Love them, lift them, reach them, teach them;
Grace of God, eternal grace, reach the lost through me.

Life of God, eternal life, pour thyself through me.
Nothing less than Thine own life do I ask of Thee.
Life compelling, life that's telling—
Life of God, eternal Life, pour thyself through me.

—L.R.

Chapter Fourteen

INTERCESSORY PRAYER

The Church has many praying men, but few men of prayer. I cannot find a place in the Scriptures where angels sing. Neither can I find a place where their praying is mentioned. Is there a connection? Is it that they cannot sing because they know nothing of the victory of prayer?

I think that the greatest privilege ever offered to man was that of sharing Gethsemane with the Lord. As we discussed in Chapter 6, Peter, James, and John were with Him, but they fell asleep. I always find this incredible! These three favored men had been with Him previously on the Mount of Transfiguration, and Luke records that there they fell asleep, also. Was it because He prayed so long that they found the going too tough for their immature spiritual lives? I would think that they would have learned a bitter lesson at the Transfiguration; but, they fell asleep again at the same event—in the prayer session of the Master! Before we castigate the disciples for this weakness and duplicate failure, let's check on ourselves. How often have we gone to sleep praying? Or how often have we given prayer the leftovers of our time, or waited until there was no other way out?

By biblical definition, great is the mystery of godliness. One might say the same thing about prayer. There is nothing mechanical about it. There is no formula.

Some time ago, I preached at a certain church; part of my interest in the people there was that they were reputedly a Spirit-filled people. My subject was a favorite of mine: "Elijah—He Prayed" and "He Prayed Again." I felt God's gracious presence as I presented the truth He had given me. But many of the people were offended! A deacon in the church was outraged. He said, "I thought you would give us five steps to the prayer life."

Before he was saved, Paul as "Saul" had a vision—"and hath seen in a vision" (Acts 9:12). After he was saved he also had a vision of a man of Macedonia. In the final manifestation of divine power foretold in Joel we read, "Your young men shall see visions" (Joel 2:28).

Let's get this straight in our thinking: no one—and I mean *no* one—is going to tell God what to do or how to do it in His final act of mercy of this age. We cannot lay a track and dare to ask Deity to comply with our stiff theology, however accurate, so that we can "accept" His manifestations. He is Lord! There will be visions, I am sure. Yet no one should seek them for the novelty of the thing. We are not told that a person is superior to another because he has visions.

My heart was stirred, my spiritual pulse quickened, when I talked privately with Duncan Campbell, so used of the Lord in what is called the Hebrides Revival. In this small group of islands off the west coast of Scotland is a place called Barvas, a village on the island of Lewis and Harris. Campbell was asked to preach there, but he could not go; he was already committed to other places. There had been powerful prayer ascending to the throne for a move of the Spirit in the place. Not the least of the intercessors, indeed some would say the most powerful of them, were two sisters, Peggy and Christine Smith. They were eighty-four and eighty-two years old respectively and spoke only Gaelic. Peggy was blind and her sister almost bent double with arthritis ("God hath chosen the weak things of the world to confound the things which are mighty"—1 Cor. 1:27).

Faith comes by hearing. These precious intercessors had grasped the promise, "I will pour water upon him that is thirsty, and floods upon the dry ground" (Isa. 44:3). This they pleaded day and night in prayer. Campbell's refusal to go to Barvas was accepted as the mind of the Lord, at least by most folks. However, Peggy, the blind prayer warrior, would have none of it. She had the promise. Her spirit, if not her voice, was saying, "I will not let Thee go until Thou bless Barvas!"

The second letter saying that Duncan Campbell could not come to the place brought this answer from her: "That's what the *man* says—*God* has said otherwise! Write again! He will be here within a fortnight [two weeks]." He went!

After Campbell had preached on the foolish virgins and come down from the pulpit, a young deacon raised his hand and, moving it in a circle over his head, said, "Mr. Campbell, God is hovering over. He is going to break through. I can hear already the rumbling of heaven's chariot wheels."

The entire congregation was lingering outside the church. Many faces showed signs of deep spiritual distress. Suddenly a young man, overburdened for the lost around him, broke out in an agonizing cry—his prayer was aflame! So overcome was he that he fell into a trance and lay prostrate on the floor. The congregation moved back into the church. Many sought the Lord. There was great grief over and repentance for sin. Now the revival was on!

While the Lord was working in the church building, Peggy and her sister were interceding at the throne. Peggy sent the following message to her minister—listen to this language, not common to our ears used to all our mass evangelism and flamboyant gospel shows:

> We struggled through the hours of the night, refusing to take a denial. Had He not promised, and would He not fulfill? Our God is a covenant-keeping God, and He must be true to his covenant engagements. Did He fail us? Never! Before the morning light broke, we *saw* the enemy retreating, and our wonderful Lamb take the field.

When asked what supported their faith in the prayer encounter, Peggy answered, "We had a consciousness of God that created a confidence in our souls which refused to accept defeat."

Yes, there is a word that says, "Touch not mine anointed, and do my prophets no harm" (1 Chron. 16:22). But what if the prophet is temporarily out of hearing of the Lord? Andrew Woolsey, the biographer of Duncan Campbell, talked of Peggy's having a holy intimacy with the Lord. How right he is. Paul said, "I withstood [Peter] to the face, because he was to be blamed" (Gal. 2:11). Peggy withstood Campbell. She had asked the preacher to come to a small, isolated village and hold a meeting. The people of that village were not in favor of the revival-type meetings. Duncan told Peggy so, and that he doubted her wisdom in this thing. She turned in the direction of his voice, her sightless eyes seeming to penetrate his soul, and said, "Mr. Campbell, if you were living as near to God as you ought to be, He would reveal His secrets to you, also."

Duncan accepted the rebuke. Then he knelt with Peggy, and the dear intercessor said, "Lord, You remember what You told me this morning, that in this village You are going to save seven men who will be pillars in the church of my fathers. Lord, I have given Your message to Mr. Campbell, and he seems not prepared to accept it. O Lord, give him wisdom, because he badly needs it."

Duncan went to the village, preaching in the large room of a house. His message was, "The times of this ignorance God winked at; but now commandeth all men everywhere to repent" (Acts 17:30). By the time he was through preaching, many were mourning for their sins—among them, Peggy's seven men!

WATCH AND PRAY

If God should turn my night to day,
It matters not one jot,
If that's His way
To teach me how to watch and pray.

If He will give to me a greater vision;
If He will grant my thoughts His own revision;
If He will give to me a broken heart;
If He will speak the word, "My son, depart,"

And I have less than
Other men to sleep,
And while they laugh
In loneliness I pray and weep,

What matters if believers think me mad?
In that Great Day, I shall not then be sad
That I had grace to softly steal away, to pray;
While others, maybe most, did idle time away.

This race is not to the swift or strong,
But to the few who fight the wrong
With revelation from His Word,
Reject Baal, and follow on to know the Lord!

—L.R.

Chapter Fifteen

THE COST OF INTERCESSION

The preacher was waxing eloquent as he portrayed the crucifixion of our blessed Lord and Savior Jesus Christ. The gen-
tle young lady sitting in front of me began to shudder, then
dropped her head into her hands. She obviously was deeply
moved. The preacher reminded us that "the crown they put on
the head of Jesus was not made of the usual type of thorns, but
they were long and not just placed upon His brow, but
rammed down, piercing the flesh, lacerating it as the blood
flowed." She shuddered again as the preacher described the
battering of the nails into His hands and His feet. She shook as
the preacher described the jamming of the cross into the
ground, thereby adding dramatic effect.

Later a number of the folks said, "That was a Roman Cath-
olic picture of the death of our Lord." The fact is that the
preacher did not come within the scope of the real factor in
telling of His magnificent death. Let Isaiah help me out here:
"When thou shalt make his *soul* an offering for sin, he shall
see his seed. . . . He shall see of the travail of *his soul.* . . . I
will divide him a portion with the great . . . because he hath
poured out his soul unto death" (Isa. 53:10-12). Maybe the dying thieves suffered physical pains as excruciating as those
that Jesus bore in the *flesh*, but they had no *soul* pains.

Again Isaiah speaks: "He bare the sin of many, and made
intercession for the transgressors" (Isa. 53:12). The divine
meaning of "intercession" is "the outpouring of the soul."
Hannah, you may remember, "prayed unto the Lord, and

wept sore." Then she continued to pray. Then she adds the awesome words: "I have drunk neither wine nor strong drink, but have *poured out my soul* before the Lord" (1 Sam. 1:10, 15). Her anguish at her barren state overcame all the scorn of the high priest who was out of touch with such intercession. The self-effacing, willing-to-be-cursed Apostle Paul knew the same depths of self-abnegation when he tells us, "Neither count I my life dear unto myself" (Acts 20:24).

A "Weekend Retreat for Intercession" is a contradiction in terms. Intercession is not a passing spasmodic thing. It is a soul passion. It is a marriage to the will of God in its deepest human expression. It is travail before triumph.

There is an interesting background to the manifest power of God during the Welsh Revival. Mrs. Jesse Penn-Lewis had been at the great Keswick Conference in the Lake District of England (1896). There she pleaded that the folks would intercede that such a conference would be born in Wales. It was born. The place of its birth? Llandrindod Wells. This conference, along with the Keswick meetings, was a power house of prayer that God used and accepted for birthing what is called the Welsh Revival. It was, of course, the *Spirit's* revival in Wales.

A similar story can be told of the New England awakening under Jonathan Edwards. Dr. John Erskine of Scotland had witnessed some explosions of divine power. He knew that this was not an operation of the flesh, so he wrote to Jonathan Edwards. The result? This blessed man, Edwards, became hungry to see the Master exalted in a great outpouring of the Spirit. This eventually occurred.

In Leeds, England, in the 1920s, we occasionally used to visit a small Pentecostal church. The pastor was, in the opinion of many, unlearned and ignorant. But he fasted often. He came near to total physical collapse on three different occasions through lengthy fasts. And the meetings in his church grew until he had to get a larger place. He, along with others, laid siege on the throne of the Lord. Had He not said, "Call unto me, and I will . . . shew thee great and mighty things"? (Jer. 33:3). Poor, laboring men prayed late into the night. They laid a prayer foundation for a great local revival. Then George Jeffreys came to town. We were warned not to go near the meetings. I went. I was hungry to be in a meeting where the preacher could say, "My preaching is not in word only, but in power and demonstration of the Holy Ghost."

In three weeks' time about three thousand people had been moved by the hand of our almighty God, and many amazing healings had taken place. The church is still there after sixty years—amazing witness to the power of God in local revival.

This move was not after a night of prayer or a seminar on the possibilities of divine invasion. But there was travail of souls, and loads of criticism and almost unbelievable opposition from those who "believed the Bible from cover to cover"—and scowled that they were left high and dry when the floods of blessing came.

The intercessor lives very close to the heart of God. He has an intimacy with the Lord of creation that few ever know. "The secret of the Lord is with them that fear him" (Ps. 25:14). The intercessor often has foreknowledge of what the Lord will do—"Shall I hide from Abraham that thing which I do?" (Gen. 18:17). How interesting! Abraham was not at the top of the social register when God was planning to overthrow Sodom. Rather, Lot was the mayor of the city, or at least an overlord, because he "sat in the gate" (Gen. 19:1), the place of local government. (To digress for a moment, does this mean that "the gates of hell" which "shall not prevail against [the Church]" (Matt. 16:18) are the headquarters of infernal powers where demons sit in counsel to thwart the purposes of God?)

Also consider Hannah. Was she in a *temporary* spot of shame? Far from it. Her adversary had tormented her for years with scorching provocation until Hannah's heart was sore. Her shame multiplied every year. Her name was a byword among her kinfolks. She had been humiliated—"Oh, you

mean the poor, barren Hannah?" This fasting, grieving, praying woman said to God, "I will not let thee go except thou
bless me." Her own soul was bitter to her taste, her own tears
were her drink. This voiceless intercessor did not pray for the
peace of Jerusalem, nor personal prosperity; she was shamed
and in the dust that she bore no child. Oh, that we might have
pastors with a heart like this, with a zeal like this, with a passion like this!

Some sixty years ago I read about a pastor who had put a
notice outside his church: "THIS CHURCH WILL HAVE
EITHER A REVIVAL OR A FUNERAL." It had a revival.
God does not answer many prayers—they are too locked-up in
self-pity or aimed at personal benefit. He does answer *desperate* prayer. Lord, teach us so to pray!

THE MARTYR'S CROWN

The saints of old were beaten, tried,
Condemned and even crucified.
These martyr men beat no retreat
When flames were licking at their feet.
They saw the tyrant's brandished steel,
But still they offered no appeal.

They struck no bargain for their lives,
For their children or their wives.
All slowly roasted in the flames
While angels wrote each of their names
Within a book God calls His own
To be proclaimed before His throne.

Then we shall know of these renown
When each receives his martyr's crown,
When God shall say to these, "Well done.
You ran the race, pressed on, and won,
When in that race men said, 'Insane.'
But now I gladly own your name.
Now you are home! Come dwell with Me
In joy through all eternity."

—L.R.

BECAUSE YOU PRAYED

God touched our weary bodies with His power,
And gave us strength for many a trying hour
In which we might have faltered
Had not you, our intercessors,
Faithful been and true.

Because you prayed,
God touched our eager fingers with His skill,
Enabling us to do His blessed will
With scalpel, suture, bandage—better still
He healed the sick and wounded, cured the ill.

Because you prayed,
God touched our lips with coals from altar fire,
Gave Spirit fullness, and did so inspire
That when we spoke, sin-blinded souls did see,
Sin's chains were broken—captives were made free.

Because you prayed,
The dwellers in the dark have found the Light;
The glad, good news has banished heathen night;
The message of the cross so long delayed
Has brought them life at last because you prayed!

—Selected

God forbid that I should sin *against the Lord* in ceasing to
pray for you.

—1 Samuel 12:23

Chapter Sixteen

THE INTERCESSORS

Would to God that every preacher in the land would at least shed his timidity, overcome his lethargy, and cry with tearful authority the words of Isaiah 59. Today we are where the Jews were when Isaiah wrote.

Occasionally there is a feeble repetition of Isa. 59:1: "Behold, the Lord's hand is not shortened, that it cannot save; neither is his ear heavy, that it cannot hear," but there we stop. Read on: "But your iniquities have separated between you and your God, and your sins have hid his face from you, that *he will not hear*" (Isa. 59:2).

Isaiah describes this evil:

"For your hands are defiled with blood, and your fingers with iniquity; your lips have spoken lies, your tongue hath muttered perverseness" (v. 3).

"They trust in vanity, and speak lies; they conceive mischief, and bring forth iniquity" (v. 4).

"Their feet run to evil" (v. 7).

"We grope for the wall like the blind, and we grope as if we had no eyes: we stumble at noonday as in the night; we are in desolate places as dead men" (v. 10).

"Our transgressions are multiplied before thee, and our sins testify against us; . . . and as for our iniquities, we know them; in transgressing and lying against the Lord, and departing away from our God" (vv. 12, 13).

"Truth is fallen in the street" (v. 14).

"And the Lord saw it, and it displeased him" (v. 15).

113

"And he saw that there was no man, and wondered that there was NO INTERCESSOR" (v. 16).

In that calamitous hour there was no man to act as an intermediary between the sin of the nation and a holy God.

The picture of the nation of which Isaiah speaks is the same as that of the nations today. One wonders what the holy Creator thinks of the complex, powerless, heavily-financed, electrified (but not electrifying), computerized system that we dare to call the "church" in this hour.

Does God still look for intercessors? Will He take the fund raisers, and the advance men, and the tireless energy of the flesh in exchange for the sweat of the intercessors?

In 1980 John White gave us his incisive book, *The Golden Cow—Materialism in the 20th Century Church*. David Lyon, in his critique of the book, wrote, "159 blistering pages." Then he gives this excerpt from the book:

> There are many so-called monuments to faith around the world today. People would like us to believe that God raised them in answer to believing prayer. I don't think so. Many are monuments to human ingenuity, to public relations know-how, to clever advertising, to skill in milking Christian suckers.

Lyon adds his own opinions:

> ". . . churches which resemble business organizations."

> ". . . our lack of awe and wonder which results from our mind-shrinking lust for things, brain-washing under the name of evangelism."

If God were looking from His holy habitation for the ploys, plays, and programs among us, He would find them prolific. But He is looking for intercessors. Where will He find them?

Intercessors are a rare breed. They are never "booked solid for the next three years." They never turn up at the national conference of any denomination—"by popular demand." The intercessor does not merely have God first in his life; for him it is *God only*. He lives, moves, and has his being in God. He loves the Lord his God with all his soul, and with all his might, *and* he loves his neighbor—that's why he is an intercessor. I read of different groups as intercessors for this country or that. But a person just spending half an hour in prayer every Friday morning for his nation knows nothing of intercession.

The command of God to Abraham was "walk *before* me" (Gen. 17:1). The children of Israel were told to "walk *after* the Lord" (Deut. 13:4). Enoch and Noah "walked *with* God" (Gen. 5:24; 6:9). But we who are members of His blessed Body have a closer walk: "As ye have therefore received Christ Jesus the Lord, so walk ye *in* him!" (Col. 2:6). The able Mr. Arthur Pink summarizes these varied aspects of the believer's walk as intimated by the four different positions thus: "We walk 'before' God as *children*; we walk 'after' Him as *servants*; we walk 'with' Him as His *friends*; we walk 'in' Him as *members* of His Body."

The intercessor's intimacy with God means that when God is hurting, he is hurting. Because he is filled with the Spirit, what grieves the Holy Spirit will grieve his spirit. The intercessor has pains to which other believers are strangers. The intercessor is the most selfless person on earth. He is impervious to social pressure. His judgments are not according to popular opinion, but based on the pressures of the Spirit within him and, in these days, the ever-present Word of God—the inerrant Bible. His spiritual pulse never slackens. His zeal for God cannot be tempered, His compassion knows no variations. He is God-appointed, God-supported, God-enlightened.

You may as well look for a man making jokes in hell as try to find an intercessor who debases the eternal, holy God by begging for money, or sending out his fund raisers or advance men.

The intercessor never loses sight of the fact that men are "by nature the children of wrath" (Eph. 2:3), and that "the wrath of God is revealed from heaven against *all* ungodliness and unrighteousness of men" (Rom. 1:18). He knows that God's wrath is nothing less than a manifestation of His indignation.

Confident of God's justice, the true intercessor holds on until the birth. He sees God, not as a master red with rage, or pale with passion and trembling on the verge of blind fury; rather, he knows that the very nature of God is love. He knows that those who reject this love, "so amazing and so divine," are opting for the awful judgment that will soon fall upon men, and for the unanswerable prayer that men will utter when trapped on the verge of eternity with no possible escape. They will cry to the mountains and rocks:

"Fall on us, and hide us from the face of him that sitteth on the throne, and from the wrath of the Lamb: for the great day of his wrath is come; and who shall be able to stand?" (Rev. 6:16, 17).

And "he that sitteth in the heavens shall laugh: the Lord shall have them in derision" (Ps. 2:4).

O God! Holy God! How many of us preachers see hell's mouth enlarged to swallow the blind and rebellious millions who at this moment are laughing their way to perdition? God anoint our sightless eyes!

RECRUITS ARE FEW

There's a burden to be lifted
And a barrier to be shifted
It would seem God's need is supermen today.
Wicked rulers in high places
Seem intent to ruin races,
While Christians make their daisy chains and play.

God has need of soldiers true.
Demons laugh. Recruits are few,
So that death and hell and Satan have their sway.
No, my son, the task's not done,
Scarcely has it yet begun.
Men—all classes—totter to the grave,
To that great eternal night; with no ray of hope in sight,
Tramp lost millions whom our Jesus died to save.

Gracious God, our hearts inspire.
Touch us with celestial fire.
Give us burning heart, and bursting lips, and brimming eyes,
Strength of purpose, power of will.
There's a place for us to fill
And a victor's crown awaiting in the skies!

—L.R.

Chapter Seventeen

FROM SAUL TO PAUL

His bodyguards stood speechless and stunned, "hearing a voice, but seeing no man" (Acts 9:7). Minutes before, their master had been charging down the highway muttering and breathing out threats against the Lord's anointed. This oppressor, blind with rage, was not plotting to overthrow the Roman persecutors; he wanted to erase the Christian liberators!

This man was no brigand—check his papers. His birth certificate says that he was "of the tribe of Benjamin, of the seed of Abraham." He was top scholar in the school of the Pharisees. His father was a Pharisee, also. He had other papers to tell you that he was "free born" and Roman by right. He could have given you an impeccable history of his people, the God-chosen of the earth. His head was full of theology, but his heart was full of hate.

The penniless, homeless prophet called Jesus had shattered the peace of Jerusalem. He had given the populace a taste of His miracle power, and by this had started a sect known as His Disciples. They, like Jesus, carried the power over disease and even over death. But the faith of Saul's fathers stood in a cloud of scorn. This man Saul would wither all the confidence of the Jesus followers. His plan, long and immaculately calculated, was foolproof. Who could withstand the authority of the signed and sealed documents concealed in his toga? Saul did have some haunting memories that shook him at times—he had agreed to and witnessed the death of a mere youth, and he saw the face of the dying youth divinely illuminated (I am sure in his sleep). But the God of Israel had been set aside; the young "Jesus men" had daringly charged the leaders of Israel with crucifying the Lord of Glory.

As he journeyed, suddenly Saul's eyes ceased to function. He was thrown to the ground crying, "Who art thou, Lord?" His bodyguard led him blind into the city of Damascus. Oh, to know what he saw during his blindness—more, I am sure, than he had ever seen in his life! Perhaps he was hounded by the bloodied faces of the people he had murdered—"many of the saints did I shut up in prison . . . and when they were put to death, I gave my voice against them" (Acts 26:10).

Guilt-laden and haunted by fearful memories, Saul collapsed in his blindness, and he prayed. The eternal God of infinite mercy heard him. Looking down from His throne to a spot in the universe called earth, God saw a finite, mistaken zealot, now confessing his spiritual bankruptcy and calling for help.

I do not read that this same mighty God sent a messenger to Caesar that day in the crowded Colosseum, or that He interrupted the schedule of the high priest, or that an angel invaded the Holy Club of the Pharisees. He visited the man on the Damascus Road because, despite his false zeal, he was hungry for God. Blessed are they that hunger.

This man Saul was a persecutor of the Faith;
soon he would be persecuted *for* the Faith.

He silently watched Stephen stoned;
soon he would be silent while he is stoned.

He put others in grave peril,
soon he would be in "perils of the deep,"
perils among his own countrymen, as well as others.

This Saul, who became Paul, was the best example of what he later wrote to the Galatians: "Whatsoever a man soweth, that shall he also reap" (Gal. 6:7).

I wish we had a record of Paul's prayers during his blindness. Oh, that every soul would have three days fasting and praying in "blindness." Try it preacher; just be "blind" to your television, video games, ball games, trivia, and even your church's social program—for three days. This is not much out of your life, but I guarantee that if God comes to you, your life will leap into realms of victory that your theology never brought you.

I wonder what Paul's bodyguards thought of their distinguished Pharisee friend as he groaned over his sins before the Lord. Maybe Paul was praying that the whole house of Israel might have a slaying before the Lord, and a wave of repentance that they had crucified the Lord of Glory.

Ananias must have been a man of prayer, also. He did not just talk to God that day, but waited until God talked to him. How seldom we do the waiting! Maybe in our own neighborhood or city there is a person to whom the Lord wants to send us, but we are too busy to wait and listen to God. Who or what takes priority over God in our lives?

Paul's finishing school was Arabia. There he was lifted up into the third heaven and given a revelation that he could not utter. Any man favored with such a revelation would come back to earth holding in contempt "all the vain things that charm us most." He would drop materialism as though it were leprosy. He would say with Paul, "This *one* thing I do" (Phil. 3:13); and, like Paul, never backslide.

Paul's prayer on the Damacus Road started a prayer chain that goes on to this day. He birthed a billion prayers there. He birthed a missionary movement unequalled to this day. He matured in prayer until he could call the blessed Holy Spirit to bear witness that he was not lying, or pretending, or fishing for praise when he cried (with tears I am sure), "For I could wish that myself were accursed [*anathema*, 'cast away'] from Christ for my brethren."

Pastor, dare you face your folks and tell them that from now on you are going to be a New Testament preacher as Paul was and do what you are ordered to do by the Spirit: "We will give ourselves *continually* to *prayer*, and to the ministry of the word"? (Acts 6:4). This will revolutionize your life and your church. If Almighty God heard a bloodstained, wicked murderer's prayer (and He did so when Paul prayed), then will He not listen to our tearful intercessions?

Jesus left His throne to intercept Paul on the Damascus Road. He will come to us in power that we have never known before when we shed all confidence in the flesh and hide our scholarly diplomas in the bottom drawer, to seek a Spirit-saturated heart with its eternity-conscious lifestyle and its demon-defying power. We have had too much of what we now have for too long. It is time for change. On the personal, congregational, and national level, we need a spiritual earthquake. Are *you* a candidate for making it happen? It is costly.

O HOLY GHOST, DESCEND!

When Thy Shekinah glory fell,
The priests stood still in awe.
Nor could the great Apostle tell
The glory that he saw
When Thou didst lift him to the sky
To sights unseen by mortal eye.

When Moses stood with unshod feet
And Thy great presence felt,
No trumpeter could call retreat
While gazing where Thou dwelt!
He listened, raptured by Thy voice,
And strangely did his heart rejoice.

The toilers' fishing nets were left
In answer to Thy call,
And worldly men with sense bereft
Before Thy feet would fall.
Those simple men Thou didst endue
With power original to You.

O Lord, we labor in a day
When men of faith are few.
Now just a remnant watch and pray.
Again we beg—endue
Thy Church with apostolic power
For true revival in this hour.

Have we the holy channel blocked
With unbelief and sin?
Have we not asked and sought and knocked
To bring the Glory in?
How is now Thy Spirit grieved
That He withholds the shower
That would revival tide bring in,
And apostolic power?

Is Thy blest holy Word unread?
Have we but ceased to pray?
Have carnal longings in our hearts
Brought spiritual decay?
Come, Thou great Physician, come,
And circumcise the heart;
Fleshly impediments remove,
And all Thy might impart.

So let the beauty of the Lord
On Christians be outpoured,
That we forget "our" ministry,
And glorify the Lord.
We hate the boasting flesh
Which often claims Thy name.
Descend, O Holy Ghost, descend
With all Thy purging flame!

—L.R.

Chapter Eighteen

GOD SOUGHT FOR A MAN,
BUT FOUND NONE

It seems that Nehemiah was raised in exile, yet he never forgot the faith of his fathers or the stories about the glory of the Lord that had been manifest before them. Josephus concluded that Nehemiah's heart was grieved because he had heard some travelers, in his own tongue, talking of the distress of the Jews in captivity. They had said:

"The remnant that are left of the captivity there in the province are in great affliction and reproach: the wall of Jerusalem also is broken down, and the gates thereof are burned with fire" (Neh. 1:3).

At this news Nehemiah did four things: (1) I sat down and wept, (2) and mourned certain days, (3) and fasted, (4) and prayed before the God of heaven (Neh. 1:4). It was not a five-minute emergency prayer; Nehemiah wrote:

"I pray before thee now, day and night" and *"O Lord, I beseech thee, let now thine ear be attentive to the prayer of thy servant, and to the prayer of thy servants"* (Neh. 1:6, 11).

Here is a man who had never seen the former glory of his nation. Likewise, we are a people who have only heard with our ears what the Lord of Glory can do in revival. We have not seen this with our eyes.

So often, God's people have refused God's visitation. From the captivity of the Jews in Babylon until their release through Cyrus, there were seventy painful years. Yet when given the chance to return, only fifty thousand responded. When Israel's spies were sent to survey the Promised Land, only two voted to enter that land flowing with milk and honey. These two saw the God of Israel and remembered that He had parted seas and delivered them from their enemies. The others saw the high walls and the tall men, and they backed off. Contrast this with Pentecost. The resurrected Jesus was seen by "above five hundred brethren at once" (1 Cor. 15:6), and I am sure they all were invited to the Upper Room to wait for that shattering experience of being filled with the Holy Ghost. Yet 380 chose not to go!

We are in a day when the walls of the house of the Lord are broken down, when our youth are more than singed with the fires of worldliness and secret sin. But few of us battle against satanic powers. Where is our heartbreak over the malignancies that bind our people today? When, oh, when did your pastor cry in a fervent prayer from the pulpit, "Oh that thou wouldest rend the heavens, that thou wouldest come down . . . (Isa. 64:1), or "My heart and my flesh crieth out for the living God" (Ps. 84:2)? Or when did he borrow the tear-stained prayer of Rachel: "Give me children or I die!" (Gen. 30:1)?

The worldlings are sailing to hell watching *The Love Boat*; the Christians are sailing to the Judgment Seat while riding "The Dove Boat"—"peace at any price." It is a deadly gospel of tolerance and compromise. How blest we think we are that we have no Pharisees today, and no Sadducees. We do have them, of course, under a new name. They blaspheme our Savior and the cross and the mighty resurrection! Read this theological garbage from Mormon "prophet," Joseph Smith:

> God, Himself, was once as we are now and is an exalted man and sits enthroned in yonder heavens. That is the Great Secret. We have imagined and supposed that God was God from all eternity. I will refute that idea. (Journal of Discourses, V6, p. 3, 1844)

We need a holy war against all false teaching and all iniquity.

First we must shut down the sanctuary and do some housecleaning, "The time is come that judgment must begin at the house of God" (1 Pet. 4:17). Then, aflame with holy passion, we should pull down strongholds through prayer. When a nation calls its prime men to battle, homes are broken, weeping sweethearts say their good-byes, businesses are closed, college careers are wrecked, factories are refitted for wartime production, rationing and discomforts are accepted—all for war. Can we do less for the greatest fight that this world has ever known outside of the cross—this end-time siege on sanity, morality, and spirituality?

Let us all lay aside every weight. Television was the great time-stealer a few years ago. Now the video machines have men, even preachers, "chained" to them. Since it would not be proper to attend certain movies, we can now have a private night club in our home and watch nudity and corruption, while the wife and children are in bed.

God begins with the spiritual *leaders*, then works down. Malachi warned, "And now, O ye *priests*, this commandment is for you. . . . I will even send a curse upon you, and I will curse your blessings: yea, I have cursed them already, because ye do not lay it to heart" (Mal. 2:1, 2). In the next chapter he stated, "But who may abide the day of his coming? and who shall stand when he appeareth? for he is like a refiner's fire, and like fullers' soap: and he shall sit as a refiner and purifier of silver: and he shall purify the sons of Levi" (Mal. 3:2, 3). Notice that He is not saying that He will purify the Amalekites or the Amorites; He will purify His *priests*!

Ezekiel cried:

"Her priests have violated my law, and have profaned mine holy things: they have put no difference between the holy and profane, neither have they shewed difference between the unclean and the clean, and they have hid their eyes from my sabbaths, and I am profaned among them" (Ezek. 22:26).

Then God spoke a heart-rending thing in the midst of this spiritual bankruptcy and spiritual misery (note verse 25 and send it to your favorite radio or television preachers). Verses

30 and 31 should be read every day for a month by every evangelical pastor in the world:

"And I SOUGHT FOR A MAN among them, that should make up the hedge, and stand in the gap before me for the land, that I should not destroy it: BUT I FOUND NONE.

"Therefore [because of this] have I poured out mine indignation upon them: I have consumed them with the fire of my wrath; their own way have I recompensed upon their heads, saith the Lord God" (Ezek. 22:30, 31).

Who is on the Lord's side? Where are the prayer warriors to fight the battle against principalities and powers, against the rulers of darkness of this world, against spiritual wickedness in high places? Who will make up the hedge and stand in the gap before God to stem the tide of iniquity in this world before He consumes us with the fire of His wrath?

Preacher!
Quit playing, start praying.
Quit feasting, start fasting.
Talk less with men, talk more with God.
Listen less to men, listen to the words of God.
Skip travel, start travail.

If you are a church leader, God will hold *you* responsible for the spiritual state of your church. Maybe it is a prayerless church because it has a prayerless pastor. Maybe it has no tears because its pastor and deacons have no tears. "Store my tears in thy bottle," says the Psalmist. I am persuaded that all the tears shed over hell-bound souls in one week throughout the entire world could be collected in one *small* bucket!

OH, LET ME DRINK THY CUP!

Prune my withered branch;
Dung my fruitless tree;
Spring up my dried-out well,
O Christ of Calvary.

Touch my dimming eyes;
Oil my stammering tongue;
Complete, dear Lord, in me
What Thou hast scarce begun.

Empower me for the load;
Wean me for Thy will;
Correct me with Thy rod;
And more I'll love Thee still.

Of Thy suffering, Lord,
I pray, Fill me up,
That I may follow Thee.
Oh, let me drink Thy cup!

—L.R.

Chapter Nineteen

PRAYER *IS* THE BATTLE

The Rolling Stones rock band rolled through America not long ago. Commenting on that tour, *Newsweek* called it a trip of "erotic exorcism for a doomed decade." These last two words have haunted me—"doomed decade." So this is what the *secular press* says about what the Bible calls "The Last Days." What "doom" do they think of? Is it a picture of the world barbecued after the world's first nuclear war?

Centuries ago Isaiah spoke of a period when "darkness shall cover the earth and gross darkness the people." I think that we are in this state right now—darkness everywhere. To make sure that the kids get used to the darkness, and lest they find out what deceivers politicians and teachers are, schools have taken the lamplight of the Bible from their feet and their path, then doped them with humanistic teachings and Darwin's "theory." The world does not believe the Bible, and the Church does not obey it. If ever there was a day when we should cry with Charles Wesley, "Oh, for a trumpet voice on all the world to call!" it is today.

Here is a word of warning from Erwin Prange's book, *A Time for Intercession*:

> The bills for the sins and indulgences of our brief history are all suddenly coming due. The party is over for the United States, with the disappearance of cheap energy. The bills for the slave ships are now being collected in the crime-ridden ghettos of our great cities. The notes for our careless wars and prodigal ways are being called in.

> In Vietnam we saw the limitations of our power; in the energy crisis, the limitations of our wealth; and in Watergate, the limitations of our morality.

He could have added, "In the unsupernatural services at our churches, we see the absence of divine manifestations, and so settle for sixty minutes of lifeless, routine performance." Is this not cause for soul grief and groaning intercession?

Since childhood, we have watched the dismantling of the great British Empire. The birthplace of Methodism, of the Salvation Army, of some of the greatest missionary societies in history, is now a leading mission field itself. A French author, Marie Claude Decamps, writing in *Le Matin* of Paris, says, "After dark, London settles into exasperation. Penniless adolescents and runaway minors grow up at the Picadilly Advice Center . . . seeking information where to eat or sleep." The writer adds, "London's 'punks' are a sad lot. These green-haired children of the recession, who for years have been singing 'No Future,' have been eclipsed by skinheads, the swastika-sporting offspring of the new England." Does anyone care?

The Editor of *The Flame* reports in his editorial:

> In just over twenty-three years more than 300 Mohammedan mosques have gone up to serve the one-and-a-half million Moslems who now live in what was once "Christian" Britain. In fact, Islam is now the second largest religion in our land. During the same period, at least 650 Anglican churches have become redundant, apart from the closure of other Protestant centers in the British Isles. To add to our abasement has come the official announcement of the building in London of the largest Hindu temple outside of India.

Where are the tearful heart-cries to God for the incredible misery in the sub-Sahara region of Africa? There are one thousand deaths a day by starvation, day after day, and month after month, until half a million people die. Drought of years has brought measureless disaster. Children with little resistance die easily. One observer wrote, "Older people are tougher and last longer, yet entire villages have been wiped out." (No news of this and similar disasters are reported by the United Nations.)

All this misery obvious, one wonders what *soul* misery these precious forgotten folks have. They need more than weekend missionaries with cameras. They need what Amy Wilson Carmichael called:

A love that leads the way,
A faith that nothing can dismay,
A hope no disappointments tire,
A passion that will burn like fire.

And yet our eyes are dry—God, pity us! Racquetball and video games are more attractive than prayer for many pastors and people. But judgment is coming!

Inequality? The report from the Lausanne Congress on World Evangelism put it this way:

Imagine that all the population of the world was condensed to the size of one village of one hundred people. In this village 67 of that 100 people would be poor; the other 33 would be in varying degrees well-off. Of the total population only 7 would be North Americans. The other 93 people would watch the 7 North Americans spend one-half of all the money, eat one-seventh of all the food and use one-half of all the bathtubs. These 7 people would have ten times more doctors than the other 93. Meanwhile the 7 would continue to get more and more and the 93 less and less.

As part of the wealthy 7 we are trying to reach as many of the other 93 for Christ as we can. We tell them about Jesus, and they watch us throw away more food than they ever hope to eat. We are busy building beautiful church buildings, and they scrounge to find shelter for their families.

While starving mothers across the world weep because their withered breasts are milkless, we are cutting up babies piecemeal in the womb by D & C's, or flushing them out in powerful salines that make the unborn fetus thrash about in agony, or vacuuming them out to be dropped in garbage cans. Were these helpless babes "predestined" to this? How many Hudson Taylors or C. T. Studds have been washed down the drain? We need more than a parade before men to solve the abortion issue. We need to close every church in the land for one Sunday and cease listening to a man so we can hear the groan of the Spirit which we in our lush pews have forgotten. We must groan for the starving of the earth and the blindness of the pagan intellectuals among us. We need to weep for the folks who parade against nuclear holocaust and yet embrace the silent holocaust of the unborn.

As we face this panorama of disaster, misery, and spiritual lostness, we need to remember what Dr. G. Campbell Morgan said more than half a century ago:

> The church patronized is the church paralyzed,
> therefore, the church in peril.
> The church persecuted is the church prayerful,
> and therefore powerful.

The Upper Room men knew of the prophecy of Joel, but they obeyed the Lord and waited—ten days of heart-searching, and, I am sure, painful exposure of their weakness. We need ten days of fasting prayer in all the churches of the world.

Prayer is the language of the poor—in spirit. Since repetition is a law of learning, let me reiterate a phrase I often use in preaching on prayer:

> The self-satisfied do not want to pray.
> The self-sufficient do not need to pray.
> The self-righteous cannot pray.

King though he was, David cried: "Bow down thine ear, O Lord, hear me: for I am *poor* and *needy*" (Ps. 86:1). And again he prayed, "This *poor* man cried, and the Lord heard him" (Ps. 34:6). The less we pray, the more we maintain an attitude of, "Lord, I can manage this alone." Peter Taylor Forsyth said it well: "We do not pray in order to live the Christian life; we live the Christian life in order to pray."

The average preacher is choosy about his appearance in the pulpit, careful about his grammar, watchful that he does not violate laws of exegesis—he is on the spot before his congregation. But what a difference in his attitude toward prayer. In most cases, his pulpit prayer is a mile wide and an inch deep. But is it more important to appear the correct preacher before the smartly dressed congregation than to appear pure and passionate before a Holy God? Did any preacher in the Bible or out of it ever cry, "Hear my sermon, O God"? Pulpit prayer should be the key to the sermon (to repeat the theme of previous chapters).

Prayer is not a preparation for the battle; it *is* the battle! The effectual, fervent prayer of the righteous preacher disarms the devil *before* the preacher gets into the pulpit. Preaching does not scare the devil (I wonder what his opinion is of most of our preaching). By prayer we put the devil out of bounds and claim the Holy Presence for the sanctuary—"Be a wall of fire round about us and the glory in the midst." Preaching is a time for public reaping after private weeping. We ascend the pulpit, deliver the heaven-breathed word, and then gather up the spoils for His glory. We set the traps in prayer, we gather the spoils after preaching.

The more men pray, the less worldly they become. The less they pray, the more worldly they become. I am, of course, speaking of professing Christians at this point.

There have been some horrendous cases, of late, of preachers falling into open sin. Glaring cases of preachers dropping their wives for another woman in which they continue their adultery and remain "popular" preachers. Others are homosexuals, some are known drunkards. These sins are not the causes of backsliding, they are the *results* of it. I am persuaded that all men who fall into open sin, or even secret sin, start their sad downfall when they *neglect prayer.* Not a man on earth can succeed in the spiritual life without a life of regular prayer.

THE VICTOR'S PATHWAY

I could not live without Thee;
My Lord, I would not try!
Earth has ten thousand pitfalls;
I never would get by!
But with Thy holy presence
And Thy promises inspired,
I tread the victor's pathway,
Dear Lord, I'm climbing higher!

—L.R.

Chapter Twenty

MORE STERN WILL GROW THE CONFLICT

Biographies are always incomplete. There are private experiences too fragrant to uncover or too raw to expose. Some facts are not known. Some parts of the story are enlarged or shrunken at the whim of the biographer. This is particularly true for the prayer life of a true believer. The person alone knows the inner, and often inexpressible, anguish of his own soul. Deep calleth unto deep. God is a Spirit; man is a spirit; and there in the spirit, subsequent to conversion, God and man hold communion. Only in the inner shrine of his heart does a man know peace, power, and prevailing prayer.

The Book says, "His sweat was as it were great drops of blood." The outer sweat of the body was a sign of the inner sweat of the soul. In the Old Testament economy, a priest was not allowed to wear wool during his priestly office exercises. Wool might make him sweat, and sweat had come because of the curse. Preachers don't seem to sweat anymore, especially in prayer.

The master artists have created tear-jerking expressions of Christ's sufferings. And yet, as I mentioned in Chapter 15, it was not His broken body that was made an offering for sin. Isaiah says, "When thou shalt make his soul an offering for sin" (Isa. 53:10).

Dr. John Duncan was professor of Hebrew and Oriental languages, New College, Edinburgh, Scotland. This man of majestic philosophical and mental powers was nicknamed "Rabbi" because of his fluency in Hebrew. He taught his class from the Hebrew of the Old Testament. One day he read to the students Isaiah 53 in Hebrew. When he came to the verse, "His soul was made an offering for sin," he remarked through his tears, "Gentlemen, it was damnation, and He took it joyfully."

I am sure that the Apostle Paul, learned in Hebrew, also did not miscalculate when he prayed that daring soul-sacrificing prayer, "I say the truth in Christ, I lie not, my conscience also bearing me witness in the Holy Ghost, that I have great heaviness and continual sorrow in my heart. For I could wish that myself were accursed from Christ for my brethren, my kinsmen according to the flesh" (Rom. 9:1-3).

What a prayer! What a man! What a preacher! What an intercessor! No wonder he says that to be a living sacrifice is but "our reasonable service." No wonder he delights in being a love slave. No wonder he rejoices that he can be crucified with Christ. Here is life:

To be "dead indeed unto sin and alive unto God."

To be intimate with God, to know His will and have the power to do it.

To be so "other-worldly" as to be living with feet on earth but heart in heaven.

To walk this sin-cursed earth, and yet be seated with Him in heavenly places.

To be despised by this snobbish, perishing world, and yet to know that, having nothing, He had all things.

Paul had more revelation than other men because he sacrificed more than other men. He saw the glories of eternity because he considered everything of this earth "but dung that I may win Christ" (Phil. 3:8).

This praying man tormented the tormentor—the devil. O God! my soul aches to see at least a *few* men each year leave the seminaries with something of this inner passion for prayer, this inner strength that is more than mental accumen.

We have never had a smarter pulpit than today, but we have never had a less powerful one.

I see the churches expanding their building facilities; increasing their office space; adding a new wing or new building for a family center, or for educational or recreational purposes; but, I say again, I *never* see a church having to increase the size of the prayer room. This, I am convinced, is because the preachers themselves are shrunken in the habit of prayer. A revival of prayer in the *pulpit* would mean a revival of prayer in the pew.

We may win the applause of men by our pulpit oratory, and build a name for ourselves as the best preacher in town when we smooth ruffled feathers, but we win the applause of *heaven* when we pray. The prostrate, blinded Saul got the attention of heaven, the ministry of a vision, and the visitation of a saint *when he prayed*. God knew Saul's name and address. He was in "the street called Straight . . . in the house of Judas . . . for behold he prayeth"—God had heard that first prayer of a man stammering out a simple petition. Saul would soon become one of the greatest prayer warriors ever—Paul.

Most of us in the United States and in some other countries are comfortable and sheltered. Have we forgotten the excruciating pain of the redeemed in countries such as Vietnam and blood-drenched Cambodia? Does it have to be headline news to get our prayer lives in gear? Are we burdened by the Spirit for those languishing and anguishing in shattered countries, wrecked economies, and a daily flood of vileness? "More stern will grow the conflict as nears the King's return." We sang this almost 70 years ago in Sunday school in England.

Combined political forces and humanists scornfully derogate the blessed Gospel in their writings and on television. The devil does not oppose the cultists because he does not fear them. He saves his venom for the *true* Church. His archenemy on earth is the body of true believers.

Years back T. Austin Sparks said:

I wonder if the Lord's people are at times really alive to the issue, and whether their prayers are always a true index of their apprehension of this thing. I believe if you and I were adequately impressed, fully alive to the tremendous issue, we could never pray mere prayers. We could never allow words to run out of our mouths, which we call praying. We should be down on our faces in a tremendous conflict on God's side against the evil menace that is seeking to devour the life of God's people. We shall never pray like that unless we are really alive to what the issue is.

CALL BACK—NEVER TURN BACK

If you are far ahead of me
Along life's winding track;
If you have real supremacy
As you carry your loaded pack;
If you have found some energy
That lets you know no lack;
Friend, tell your secret now to me,
I ask you, please call back!

Some who went ahead of me
Endured thumbscrew and rack,
In biting pain they felt it gain,
Yet endured and turned not back.
They were sawn asunder, torn in two,
On their bodies beaten black.
But they went the last mile
With a song and a smile
For the One who turned not back!

Now let me tell
Of the living hell
Some saints endure today,
To be tied in a sack
Or stretched on the rack
Would seem an easier way.

But they die by the inch,
And they do not flinch
As they tread their prison track;
And they inwardly sing
To Christ their King
That they'll never, no *never*, turn back!

It's a steep, rough road
That leads to God.
We must climb its hill with a will
To carry our load
On the toughest road—
His purpose to fulfill.

There may be strain,
There may be pain,
And the food may seem "hardtack."
But He made it plain,
There's eternal gain
For the one who turns not back!

—L.R.

Chapter Twenty-one

BEHOLD, HIS NAIL PRINTS!

Preachers often make reference to Isaiah's vision in chapter six, forgetting that he began the first chapter, verse one, speaking of his vision. Why do we leap over this to get to chapter six? Is it too much like our own history and present folly? I am persuaded that the prophet cried, "Woe is me" because he saw his utter inability to reach the nation in its present rebellion and sin. His later cry, "Oh that *thou* wouldest rend the heavens!" is an admission that human effort is bankrupt.

Read what the prophet says of his nation;

"Ah sinful nation, a people laden with iniquity, a seed of evildoers, children that are corrupters: they have forsaken the Lord, they have provoked the Holy One of Israel unto anger, they are gone away backward" (1:4).

"Your country is desolate [no breath of revival upon it], your cities are burned with fire [the fires of lust]: your land, strangers devour it in your presence [the cultists and gurus]" (1:7).

"Hear the word of the Lord, ye rulers of Sodom [We now have millions of homosexuals and lesbians]" (1:10).

"I will hide mine eyes from you: yea, when ye make many prayers, I will not hear: your hands are full of blood [abortions?]" (1:15).

Now check and see if we are in the state that Israel was when Isaiah cried for divine intervention. My gifted friend, Charles Duncombe, writing in *Christ for the Nations* magazine (June 1982), has this horrendous thing to tell us:

Martin Container Service of Wilmington, California, is a standard garbage removal company. Their routine job is to dispose of the tons of debris daily accumulated by our can-fed, package-fed, snack-fed civilization. Recently the workers were instructed to remove and scour a 20-foot-long container to be removed from the Medical Analytic Lab., Inc.

This is what they found: Medical waste and hundreds of fetuses, some more than five months developed with expressions on their faces. The fetuses, pathological lab specimens, cancerous growths and confidential records of patients from San Francisco, Sacramento and Missouri were stacked eight feet high in the metal container. According to the San Pedro, California, *News Pilot*, patient names were printed on the plastic jars containing the fetuses, which were preserved in formaldehyde.

The newspaper also reported that Planned Parenthood organizations in Missouri and California, Inglewood (CA) General Hospital and several free clinics were the source of the pathological specimens dating to 1979.

Not aware of the contents of the container, the workmen were so horrified, physically revolted, and shocked by the contents that they were unable to do the job.

The large fetuses, weighing more than three pounds, were in one-gallon ice-cream type containers. The smaller ones were in jars marked "dentures."

God ordered Israel to exterminate the Canaanite tribes and cities. Contrary to the criticism that such a mandatory command was cruel and unjust, the spade of the archaeologist has uncovered a sound reason for the severity of the Divine decree. In excavations at Gezar, under the ruins of a high place built for the worship of the goddess Ashtoreth, an enclosure 150' × 120' surrounded by a wall was found. Here the inhabitants held their religious festivals. Great numbers of jars containing the remains of children were found under the debris. The whole area proved to be a cemetery for newborn babies. ("Conscienceless Culture")

How long will God wink at our "civilized iniquity" (of which Bro. Duncombe writes) in a Bible-reading nation? Best-selling author Thomas Robbins wrote a book entitled *Another Roadside Attraction*, "in which the mummified body of Jesus Christ is discovered adorning a roadside zoo and a hot-dog stand." Robbins forgot that one day he will stand before the Majestic Risen Christ to account for this blasphemy.

One expects opposition and ridicule from the worldly-wise. They equate Jesus with Buddha and other founders of religion. But what about the "pros" in the Christian religion? The men who are supposed to guide others "into all truth"? Here is a report of a survey of 10,000 Protestant *ministers* conducted by Sociologist Jeffrey Hadden; 7,441 responded to the questions.

Here are the horrifying statistics. Read them, then wonder why God is grieved with our spiritual life. (I am indebted to *Christ for the Nations*, May 1982, for this information.)

Jesus born of a virgin?

60% of Methodists said "No"
49%of Presbyterians said "No"
44% of Episcopals said "No"
19% of American Lutherans said "No"

Jesus the Son of God?

82% of Methodists said "No"
81% of Presbyterians said "No"
89% of Episcopals said "No"
57% of American Lutherans said "No"

Bible—inspired Word of God?

82% of Methodists said "No"
81% of Presbyterians said "No"
89% of Episcopals said "No"
57% of American Lutherans said "No"

Existence of Satan?

62% of Methodists said "No"
47% of Presbyterians said "No"
37% of Episcopals said "No"
33% of Baptists said "No"
14% of American Lutherans said "No"

146

Physical resurrection of Jesus?

51% of Methodists said "No"
35% of Presbyterians said "No"
30% of Episcopals said "No"
33% of Baptists said "No"
13% of American Lutherans said "No"

Here Christ is wounded in the house of His friends, the Spirit is grieved, and God the Father insulted.

In the light of this sometimes sad, sometimes sordid information, please read and digest my friend Kay Kilgore's essay, "Enjoy Yourself." Then decide whether you are living with eternity's values in view or are just being comfortable in a cocoon of selfishness. "Awake to righteousness, and sin not; for some have not the knowledge of God: I speak this to your shame" (1 Cor. 15:34).

ENJOY YOURSELF

Just live your life—and "Enjoy yourself!" Enjoy yourself—while pain lurks behind every face, and murder smolders in the hearts of men as they sit behind buttons of annihilation waiting for a justifiable moment to destroy great masses of human life.

Enjoy yourself—while the ghettos fill up and the junkies walk the streets, even children, selling themselves and their souls for the next chemical hit into their bodies and minds.

Enjoy yourself—while the unresolved conflicts, turmoils, and unanswered questions of a people fill them with emotional pain, relieved only by the dulling of their senses by drugs and other forms of escape.

Enjoy yourself—while the greedy men who consume the natural resources and wealth of the world not only take food out of the mouths of those less competitive, but now flush the sewers of polluted air down the throats of children as contaminated particles of materialism funnel into humanity.

And as we enter into these troubled times, we stand as a new generation to give a contribution to this planet. With what inane song shall we serenade the dying people? What tribute shall we give to the lusts of past generations? What morsel of meat shall we take in exchange for the hope of a new world?

Shall we succumb to the broken values of selfishness and greed again? Selfishness begets selfishness as one generation instills greed and self-seeking into the next. Will we even sell out each other for personal gain or pleasure?

What shall awaken the death shroud of a planet worshipping *self*? What shall shake the complacent and cold? Even in death they proudly take their places in padded caskets left to decay in the mold of earth, the lowest of elements.

Our stay on earth is temporary; every step we take is borrowed. Every breath we breathe could be our last. How long are we going to laugh it off and sleep it off? Isn't our hope greater than our hangups?

We find ourselves ensnared by our own inward decadence. Yet beyond the cords of selfishness and the net of vanity and fleshly pleasure stands a reality awaiting those who can lay aside the lust of the moment for the joy of the tomorrow—the hope that the flower of love and peace can still bloom even amidst the stagnation of many generations.

Every voice is coming through the night in despair and sadness. Every sound is a sob coming from the gasps of a dying world. Despair stares coldly from every face; feet stumble in the crooked paths tangled in the vines of deception.

Pride, its face twisted and sinister as filth, pours forth its gaudy ointment for the last time. What can "they" do when things really fall in? What new pill will they push to you as the answer to the problem? What new sensual pursuit can they offer you to spin your web to nowhere and wile away the hours of your existence?

Just live your life—and enjoy yourself! Your pleasures will fade into yesterdays that fade into nothingness. The selfishness of man scoffs at the hand of giving without getting; it re-

viles the heart of love that reaches out to a dying world—
BEHOLD HIS NAIL PRINTS!

Much of this chapter shows us that the world is a pigpen, surrounded by a Church that too often is a playpen. The life-blood of nations is drained by the Mafia. Colleges are corrupt. Venereal disease alarms the sociologists—they speak more of it than do the preachers. Magazines tell how, in many places of the world, nudity is allowed on the beaches. Yet amid all this, the glittering evangelism of this day, powdered with Hollywood-styling, "rich and increased with goods" (except for a little more begging), is just "wretched, and miserable, and poor, and blind, and naked." I think that preachers are guilty of criminal negligence when they cloud the real message of salvation.

The August 1982 issue of *Pulpit Helps* contains this statement: "In a recent survey of one of the large, well-known theological colleges of the United States, 93% of the students studying for the ministry stated: 'I have no devotional life.'" What a crop of future preachers! How can a man speak for God if he does not walk with God? Maybe right here I should mention a simple but searching statement of Napoleon's: "There is no greater immorality than to occupy a place that you cannot fill." Are we preachers filling and fulfilling the blessed ministry for which the Lord of Glory has appointed us?

Preacher and pew dweller, I beg you to quit blurring your spiritual vision with television. Get to bed early at night, rise early in the morning. God promises to be as dew to Israel. Dew does not fall at midday. Be an early riser. Late nights and late rising are a modern scourge for preachers. The great men of God were like Joshua who rose early in the morning.

In 1607 William Gouge was ordained to the ministry. A year later he became pastor of the church at Blackfriars, London, England. There he labored for over 45 years. For 35 of those years he preached a midweek sermon on Hebrews. A biographer wrote: "Being very conscious of how he spent his time, he always would rise early, long before daylight, and would have completed his devotions by 4 a.m." And what a prayer warrior was Gouge—"His confessions were accompanied with brokenness of heart, self-abhorence. . . . In petition he accompanied faith with fervor. . . . He, like a true son of Jacob, wrestled with tears and supplications, resolving not to let God go without a blessing."

What of the renowned John Quicke? "He was a good scholar and an animated and successful preacher. In his days of health, he used to be in his study by 2 a.m."

Then there was Robert Bruce, "that saintly preacher, favored beyond most with near approaches to God in prayer." John Livingstone, staying at the home of Bruce, said, "I saw him come from his closet with his face swollen with weeping. He had been praying for Dr. Alexander Leighton, who was pilloried in London, and for himself that he had not been counted worthy to suffer!"

William Guthrie was one of the most graceful, elegant, accomplished preachers that Scotland has ever possessed. "To say that he was admired and loved by Rutherford is almost enough. His prayers were such that whole assemblies were melted into tears. Samuel Rutherford was one of the most learned men of his age. He commonly rose at three in the morning."

After reading of their prayer habits, can you wonder that these men plumbed the depths of the Sacred Page far more deeply than we pathetic pulpiteers? No man can be a giant in prayer and a weakling in ministry.

Dr. Martyn Lloyd-Jones told me personally that he found exposition delightful, but prayer always difficult. The great Martin Luther said the same thing:

It is a tremendously hard thing to pray aright, yea, it is verily the science of all sciences, even to pray that the heart may approach unto God with all gracious confidence, and say: "Our Father, which art in heaven"! For he who can take to himself such confidence of grace is already over the hill. Difficulty has laid the foundation stone of the temple of prayer.

Jonathan Edwards, in his memoirs, wrote, "I was almost always in ejaculatory prayer wherever I was. Prayer seemed to be natural to me, as the breath by which the inward burnings of heart had vent."

In the classic diary of Andrew Bonar, we find this elevating expression: "I would never lose sight any hour of the Lamb in the midst of the throne, and if I have this sight, I shall be able to pray."

Will we ever hearken to these masters of prayer? Will we ever attempt to follow them into the secret place of the Most High?

IN HEATHENDOM

Millions are waiting yet
   In heathendom.
Will they the Gospel get
   In heathendom?
Who will arise and go
Out to this sin, this woe,
And Christ the Saviour show
   To heathendom?

The sun will soon be set
   O'er heathendom.
But they are waiting yet
   In heathendom.
Lost in the fog of sin,
Will none these wanderers win
For Jesus Christ our King
   From heathendom?

Will someone lead the way
   To heathendom?
Will others join the fray
   In heathendom?
Lord, raise a holy band
With hearts empowered to stand
All that You will demand
   For heathendom.

                    —L.R.

Chapter Twenty-two

WE PLEAD OR WE PERISH

Since the first day that Communism was born, its cheap jibe against Christianity has been, "It's pie in the sky when you die." Now we are hearing much from a people who as Christians say, "It's pie on your way to the sky." These interpreters of the spiritual life offer an experience in grace that is a summer without any winter, a rose without any thorns, a sea without any storms, a bliss without any battles. They are totally anti-biblical in this interpretation.

Jacob's famous night of wrestling in spiritual power saw him changed into a prince with God—it also brought him a limp! Samson had the most blessed of all gifts known to men—"the Spirit of the Lord came mightily upon him" (Judg. 14:6), but there was a lion in the deal, too. Our blessed Lord cried, "The spirit of the Lord is upon me." He never ministered until the anointing came, but with it came the forty days of massive temptation. Pentecost saw the Upper Room disciples transformed, and immediately after came a storm of persecution. Heads rolled, but the believers did not fold—they flamed: "We ought to obey God rather than men!"

It's time to leave the "prayer" breakfast and banqueting circuit for the battlefield. We have feasted long enough; now is the time to fast and to fight. We have clapped hands long enough; now we must let those hands cling to the sword of the Spirit as we battle against principalities and powers. The hours ahead of us will demand a showdown of strength. The underpinning of truth—the Bible is the infallible, inerrant, indestructible Word of the Lord—is being eaten away in the seminaries and schools by the acid rationalism of so-called intellectual progress. Such a battle for the Bible is not won in the lecture halls. It is won in the prayer closet.

From every pulpit we should hang this boldly written text: "For the nation and kingdom that will not serve thee shall perish; yea, those nations shall be utterly wasted" (Isa. 60:12).

It took ten vicious plagues to shake Pharaoh from his grip on Israel. Will it take ten plagues to shake us from our materialistic complacency and our spiritual sleep? Must God rain fire from heaven upon us to stop our mad rush to the fires of hell?

"While men slept the enemy sowed the tares." While we sleep in the church the devil sows his tares, sets his snares, and weighs folks down with cares. Folks heed the politicians more than the preachers these days. Materialism has mesmerized us, and we count our calories more often than we count our blessings.

Time is running out on us, liberties are drying up. Privacy is withering. Soon there will be no private holding of funds. Federal peeping at bank holdings is very near. I am told of a millionaire who, after the invasion of his country by the Communists, looked back at his once-prosperous material empire saying daily, "I wish I had used that money for the Lord." Shall we sigh that way?

God has said that He will yet shake the heavens and the earth, the sea and the dry land. The earth *is* the Lord's; let no man or government forget it. He will not always chide, neither will He keep His anger forever. Yes, He loved Israel; and He delivered Israel into the hands of the Midianites, also.

The web of impurity tightens alarmingly around the nations. The cup of iniquity is filling rapidly. Darkness covers the earth and gross darkness the people. We are contesting now against the rulers of the darkness of this world, with the unfruitful works of darkness obstructing our every step. We believers have been called out of darkness into His most marvelous light—"Ye brethren are not in darkness." In His light we see light. We see what the world cannot see either in blessing or in cursing—coming judgment.

Two world wars did not shake the world as it is being shaken at this moment. Will the Church sleep on while mankind heads for the rapids? A long-suffering God cannot wink at our iniquity much longer. He lets men go so far and then, as they announce their triumph, He intervenes.

Belshazzar had it all wrapped up. He defiled the temple vessels; he defied God; he deified himself. And when the party was a roaring success, when the flesh strutted and the people acclaimed him the greatest—then he saw the hand writing on the wall. This changed the frivolity into fear. The wine became bitter, the fun a farce, the song changed into a sigh. The wizards, the soothsayers, the astrologers and wise men could not read the warning. Then entered God's man, Daniel. He made the correct interpretation: "God hath numbered thy kingdom, and finished it. . . . Thou art weighed in the balances, and art found wanting" (Dan. 5:26, 27).

The king at another period was shaken by dreams. Again the smart men were speechless, but Joseph got through to the king with his message from the visions. (Have we already had our seven years of plenty?)

It was when all hope was gone that Paul, the brave preacher-prophet—whose prophecy of the coming blast had been ignored—stepped into the tearful mob to say, "Peace and safety if ye abide in the ship."

Isaiah spoke of a day when "a man shall be as a hiding place from the wind, and a covert from the tempest; as rivers of water in a dry place, as the shadow of a great rock in a weary land." This is just what the prophets are in the crisis hours of history.

God made the Assyrians the rod of His anger (Isa. 10:5, 6). He sent them against the hypocritical nation of Israel. Who or what will be His rod against our generation? A total collapse in the national economies? A foreign invader? More earthquakes and devastating floods? More plagues, such as the incurable "gay plague" acquired by homosexuals (Acquired Immunity Deficiency Syndrome, AIDS) from which almost half the victims die? Will God deal with our sins as He dealt with the sins of Sodom, or will He just let us rot a little further? It is a fearful thing to fall into the hands of the living God. "It is a more fearful thing to fall out of those hands," said Robert Louis Stevenson.

Before you hang your harp on the willows, before you say, "How can we sing the Lord's song in a strange land?" let me tell you, *there is a way out*! The way out of this sinful mess is: *Down* on our knees; then *up* through the skies in intercession; then *out* to the world, fire-baptized in concern, compassion, and conquest for the final outpouring of mercy before the day of His wrath.

The way out of this awesome sin plague certainly is *not* by human strategy. Despite more money spent on education in the last twenty-five years, we are lower in morality than ever before. Despite more peace pacts, pledges, and promises, we have more money invested worldwide in war machines than at any other point in history. Despite our progress in science, we face famine on the largest scale ever, right at this moment. Despite more money spent on church buildings, our spiritual birthrate is lower than ever.

Which way then? *God's* way! "*Not* by might [strength of armies], nor by power [scientific know-how and education], but *by my spirit*, saith the Lord" (Zech. 4:6). The world knows not the Spirit. He does not invade carnal hearts. We believers are His channel.

God has said, "The yoke shall be *destroyed* because of the anointing" (Isa. 10:27). This is the secret—the anointing! It is:

The enduement of power from on High—Pentecostal power—unearthly power to shake the earth.

Divine equipment to shake the strongholds of hell on earth.

Enduement to harass the devil and his powers.

Power to break the yoke from the millions bound in superstition and occult practices, manacled by drugs, enslaved by drink, locked in lust.

Power to storm heathendom with the cry of deliverance.

Power that will cripple the cults and set the captives free.

Power that will cover *His* name with glory!

Jesus is coming for a Bride, not for a widow, not for a sick Church. He is worthy to receive honor and glory and power now and forever. Against this present world's onslaught of iniquity, the race is not to the swift nor the battle to the strong. Here the lame take the prey and to those who have no might, He increaseth strength. He who heard the cry of Elijah from Carmel and of Jonah from the belly of hell will hear our cries for mercy and revival. "Call upon *me* and I *will* answer thee." We plead or we perish!

THE REVIVAL SONG

Lord, we are hungry for blessing,
This is in tune with Thy Word;
Now as our need we're confessing,
Give us new hearts, cleansed and stirred.

Great is the need of our nations,
Great is the need of this hour.
Lord, we abhor our stagnation,
Answer with Holy Ghost power.

Look on our great desperation;
Hold back Thy judgment we pray.
Move through the length of our nation;
Open Thy windows today.

Lord, fill the Church with Thy Spirit.
Lord, save our nation we pray.
Quicken our love and our zeal, and
Send us *revival* today!

—L.R.

EPILOGUE

A day of the ministration of the Spirit would bring many rare and rich blessings along with it, such as discoveries of the Redeemer's glory, convictions of the evil and vileness of sin, many crowns of victory and triumph to Christ, great additions to his friends and followers. Then gospel-light would shine clear, saving knowledge increase, ignorance and error vanish, riches of free grace would be displayed, and Satan be bound up. Then ministers and ordinances would be lively, secure sinners would be awakened, dead souls would live, hard hearts would be melted, strong lusts subdued, and many sons and daughters born to God. Such a day would heal divisions, cement breaches, make us all of one heart and mind, and bring down heaven to earth. This would redress our grievances, remove our complaints, and unite Christ's scattered flock. It would make true religion and holy persons to be in esteem, vice to be in disgrace, and iniquity as ashamed to hide its face. Then sabbaths and communions would be days of heaven. Prayer and praise, spiritual converse, talking of Christ and redeeming love, would be our chiefest delight. Oh, then, pray for such a time.

John Willison
The Balm of Gilead, 1742